"Fro[...] [de]termining whether your idea is best for 'stage, [...] wor[...], *Could It Be a Movie? – How to Get an Idea Out of Yo[...]* grounded with super, real-time advice on how to evaluate, enha[...] for big-time Hollywood!"

— **Kathie Fong Yoneda**, Script Consultant, Seminar Leader
Author: *The Script-Selling Game*

"The single most important thing about a screenplay is the basic concept. And the single most important thing aspiring screenwriters can do is read this book before they start writing."

— **Pamela Wallace**, Academy Award Winner: *Witness;* Published Author

"Hamlett's humor, conversational style, and wealth of publishing and production anecdotes make *Could It Be a Movie?* a 'must-buy' for every aspiring screenwriter. Where else can you get the hands-on advice of a novelist, playwright, screenwriter, columnist, and PR consultant all in one book? It's as if she's sitting across the table from you on every page and encouraging you to put your best script forward."

— **Eric Lilleør**, Publisher/Editor-in-Chief: *Screentalk* Magazine

"Aspiring screenwriters, start here! Before investing your time and dollars trying to coax that script onto paper, check here to find out if your idea will pass muster. Filled with practical tips and great resources and written by a top-notch author and screenwriter, this book is a delight."

— **Jenna Glatzer**, Editor-in-Chief: *AbsoluteWrite.com*

"An absolute must-read."

— **Marie Jones**, Book Reviewer: *Bookideas.com*

"If the idea is maybe a winner, then *Could It Be a Movie?* is a yardstick for making the creative process a little easier. Hamlett devises solid methods for estimating whether concepts and storylines will translate into successful feature films. A very good read for reviewing projects in the planning stages."

— **Ross Otterman**, *Directed By* Magazine

"Yes, this is primarily a book about writing for the silver screen, but it belongs on every writer's bookshelf. *Could It Be a Movie?* is a treasure chest of useful information about plot, character, dialogue, and developing the instinct to know the difference between a great idea and a mediocre one. Hamlett is a seasoned pro whose friendly, yet down-to-earth, no-nonsense advice both new and seasoned writers will turn to again and again."

— **Liz Preston**, Editor: *Plays*, the drama magazine for young people

"If you think that you have a movie in you, this book is a must-read."

— **Linda Bauer**, Author, Columnist, Lecturer

"Indispensable... packed with facts, examples, interviews with insiders, and innumerable resources, this book covers the whole journey, and not only guides but inspires with tremendous examples, both personal and professional. It speaks to the needs of many pursuing their dreams in this business: writers, actors, filmmakers, producers, and anyone who wants insight into how to become a part of the magic."

— **David Grad**, Actor: *Small Things Remembered, Hide and Seek, Follow the Leader*; Host of TCI Syndicated Series: *Power Mixx*

"I never thought there would be room for yet another how-to book on script writing until I read Christina Hamlett's *Could It Be a Movie?* Here is not someone just turning the same commonplace advice over and over again but rather a truly knowledgeable pro who supports you all the way through the process of getting your idea out of your head and on to the silver screen. The depth of her insight even allows you as a reader to delineate your own personalized trail to fame and fortune, depending on your temperament, experiences, and personal idiosyncrasies."

— **Janne Wallin**, Writer/Executive Producer: *Aristoteles AB* Feature Films: *Beck, Sprängaren/The Bomber, Festival*

"Christina provides critical insight into the real world of screenwriting in a comprehensive and entertaining way. This book is not only a catalytic spark for those screenwriters in a slump, it is the step-by-step manual for those aspiring screenwriters who need that extra push to make the commitment to pen and paper. Don't just read this book... TAKE IT TO HEART AND APPLY IT."

— **Daren N. Afshar**, Producer: Winery Productions (Japan) Producer: *Changing Worlds, Red Shadow, Pride*

"If you are, like this writer, a film junkie, then you're already a dreamer. And if you're also a writer, then the likelihood is that you dream of writing The Great American Screenplay – or at least something that won't send your hoped-for agent into spasms of derision before he or she can wrestle the metal clamp off the manuscript. It's enough in life to find someone who has been-there, done-that in the positive sense. It's a windfall to find someone like Hamlett who has been-there, done-that, and is willing to share. If *Could It Be a Movie?* isn't the screenwriter's bible, it's the toolkit. Buy it. Then, when it all finally happens, make sure they spell your name correctly in the final credits."

— **Terry Boothman**, Author: *The Writer's Software Companion* Editor/Publisher: *Writer Online* Magazine

"Christina Hamlett's is the voice of experience and reason as she shares a wealth of information with writers working on getting their stories from ideas to finished screenplays."

— **Amy Andrews**, Book Reviewer: *AbsoluteWrite.com*

COULD IT BE
a movie?

HOW TO GET YOUR IDEAS OUT OF YOUR HEAD
AND UP ON THE SCREEN

CHRISTINA HAMLETT

Published by Michael Wiese Productions
11288 Ventura Blvd, Suite 621
Studio City CA 91604
Tel. (818) 379-8799
Fax (818) 986-3408
mw@mwp.com
www.mwp.com

Cover Design: Johnny Ink
Layout: Gina Mansfield
Editor: Arthur G. Insana

Printed by McNaughton & Gunn, Inc., Saline, Michigan
Manufactured in the United States of America

© 2005 Christina Hamlett

Library of Congress Cataloging-in-Publication Data

Hamlett, Christina.
  Could it be a movie? : how to get your ideas out of your head and up on the screen / Christina Hamlett.
      p. cm.
  Includes filmography.
  ISBN 0-941188-94-9
  1. Motion picture authorship. I. Title.
  PN1996.H287 2005
  808.2'3--dc22

                                                    2004009598

With love and appreciation to
Shonali Burke, Sandy Koffman, Heather Mercer,
Liz Preston, Peggy Sugarman, and Kathie Fong-Yoneda
— a half-dozen exceptional wordsmiths
who have not only raised the bar
and continuously challenged me to keep up with them
but whose collective integrity
has placed them among my most treasured circle of friends

❧

To my husband Mark,
who never fails to remind me of the importance of
enjoying the journey as much as the destination

❧

And to my mentor,
the late Sylvia K. Burack,
who, to this day, continues to look over my shoulder
and remind me not to take shortcuts
on the things that count

TABLE OF CONTENTS

FOREWORD

On any given night, you probably can hear it if you listen closely. It's the spin of an unfettered imagination... the soft whir of a computer as it comes to life... the tentative tap of fingertips on a keyboard, slowly at first, then building in excited momentum. It's the wondrous birth of an idea whose affirmation one day will come in the grandest gift of all — the sound of applause.

The only thing it's waiting for is You.

A wise person once said "Sometimes you have to believe in something before you can see it." Such is the case with screenwriting. It begins with an idea and a blank piece of paper. With hope, smart dialogue, well-paced action, meaningful scene transitions, and characters who jump off the page follow closely behind. The reality of things is that the process of writing is probably the easy part of being a screenwriter; writing admirably is much more difficult and getting your work discovered is challenging, to say the least. But it all can be done; it happens everyday.

So let's start at the beginning with you, the writer. First and foremost, maximize your passion to write and believe that you can follow through on all that is required to reach your goals. Why is this so important? Because your desire to craft a story by means of a feature film or television script is a magical and marvelous contribution to the world. But take notice that this contribution carries with it an awesome responsibility, since it is through the written words found between "Fade In" and "Fade Out" that you get the proverbial ball rolling in the first place. Without a script, many entertainment industry people would be out of work. Actors, directors, producers, agents, and technical support staff would spend their time standing around saying, "Well now what do we do? We don't have a script from which to work. Can anybody here write a multi-layered story with 16 characters and sizzling dialogue, and don't forget the red herrings and plot points?" Succinctly put, screenwriters and the vibrant stories they tell are the lifeblood of the film industry.

So whether your script is for television or the big screen, what matters is your dedication to breathing in all the screenwriting knowledge and skills you can. There are definitely a lot of people who can write well, but the truly great screenwriter is one who learns everything he or she can about "being a screenwriter." Proper formatting, solid storytelling, believable dialogue, well-timed plot twists, and an understanding of how the business operates do more than help make a solid script, they demonstrate to the world your grasp of the art of screenwriting and your commitment to satisfying the audience's quest for vicarious escape.

And that leads us to this book, *Could It Be A Movie*. I know you will find it a great resource in your professional growth as a screenwriter, because Christina has culled essential screenwriting information and integrated it with her wise industry counsel, both of which will get you pointed in the right direction toward becoming a cinematic success and keep you there, once you've arrived.

Enjoy the book and keep writing... always keep writing!

John E. Johnson
Executive Director
American Screenwriters Association

INTRODUCTION

Movies. No matter their theme, budget or cast, they all start out in pretty much the same way. They start out with dreamers — just like you — sitting in darkened theaters around the world and imagining what it would be like to see their names scrolling up the credits after the words, "Screenplay Written By... "

Is there a movie inside of you that's been yearning to get out but didn't know how to emerge?

The exciting news is that 21st century technology and the proliferation of independent film studios have increased the newcomer's accessibility to the bright lights of Hollywood. Chat rooms, film camps, online classes, local access stations, and trade magazines abound with insider tips, techniques, and hands-on opportunities that were previously the purview of a select community. If you've always wanted to write for the movies or television, there's never been a better time for it than right now!

So how do you know if your concept is worth developing into a full-fledged script? Or, for that matter, how do you know whether the medium of film could be a comfortable fit for your own creative vision?

There are a number of excellent resource books that teach you what to say and do between FADE IN and FADE TO BLACK. This one, however, is the road map you need *before* you embark on that journey. Why? Because half the fun of your ultimate destination is all the brainstorming, preparation, and networking that go into it.

This text also allows you to explore alternative routes of putting your story and characters in front of the public. The references and comparisons to popular stage plays and novels which you will find sprinkled throughout these chapters will hone your skills at identifying whether your plot is adaptable to multiple venues, thus expanding your repertoire and career opportunities as a writer.

How do you tell the difference between mediocre ideas and great ones? This book shows you how you can put them to the test prior to a full-fledged commitment of time, energy, and paper. It even addresses those quirky, subjective elements of the craft over which even the best-intentioned writer has absolutely no control: reader bias, world events, and, yes, even human attention spans.

Should you tackle your first script on your own, team up with a writing buddy, or engage the services of a seasoned professional? Within these pages, you'll discover that the pros and cons of collaboration have more to do with personality and intuition than with actual process and substance.

And what about agents? While it's entirely possible to get through the front door without one, the right partnership can assist you in conquering the entire neighborhood. In the meantime, a user-friendly primer on the ethics and legalities of the script-selling business reveals the tandem responsibility inherent in delivering a solid story and a professional promise.

Remember, there is no one sure-fire road to success, whether it be in screenwriting or any other endeavor. There are, however, two common denominators that separate those who will reach the finish line and those who will spend a lifetime wistfully gazing at it through binoculars; specifically, perseverance, and passion. So the next time you're in the theater and say to yourself, "I could do this," start reading this book, start writing that story, and stay with it all the way!

SECTION 1

DREAMING IT UP

CHAPTER 1 | IT ALL BEGINS WITH AN IDEA

"Lights!" "Camera!" "Action!"

Before any of these commands can be shouted on a soundstage, somebody's got to come up with a great idea that everyone else will want to be a part of. Whether their jobs are to cry on cue, focus the camera, or ensure that none of the paychecks bounces, they are all in the picture because of one person — the screenwriter whose imagination gave them an exciting starting point.

Could that person be you?

In this section, you'll not only discover what skills are required to write a screenplay for today's market but also what kind of factors dictate which ideas get gobbled up faster than a holiday turkey and which ones go the way of a fruitcake.

IS THERE A SCREENPLAY IN YOUR FUTURE?
Dillinger robbed banks because that's where the money was. He also died in a hail of gunfire when he was only 31. This cautionary tale is to remind you to check your motivation before starting this journey. Many aspiring writers tend to view Hollywood in much the same way as the Depression-era bandit did banks — just there for the taking. And who can blame them? When they see the million plus dollar salaries that today's top actors and actresses command, the idea of selling to the movies sounds like a much more lucrative gig than hawking poetry chapbooks or novellas.

"Selling," of course, is the operative word. Just like Dillinger, you still need a plan to break in.

The first thing to ask yourself is why you want to.

A strange question?

Not really. Too often, the glamour of myth can cloud personal judgment in picking the best career path for anyone's talents. Furthermore, a fixation on the end-product of wealth, popularity, and good tables at restaurants ignores the unique joy that comes from the creative process. In other words (with apologies to the U.S. Navy), it's not just a job: it's an adventure.

Take the entire mystique of the screenwriter's job itself. If your impression of being a wordsmith to the stars revolves around quaffing champagne, scarfing bon-bons, and doing power lunches, you've been watching far more movies than you've been writing. The truth of the matter is that screenwriting is a workaday job pretty much like anything else and prone to a comparable level of stress, criticism, and insecurity. In fact, it probably bears uncanny similarity to whatever day-job you're holding down now.

The promise of a paycheck, for instance, depends on your performing a specific assignment and demonstrating its worth to the organization. Your work product is constantly subject to deadlines, delays, review, procrastination, censure, and revision. Furthermore, it could be years before your dedication is ever recognized and rewarded by someone who is in a position to change the status quo.

Where the path diverges is in the perception of whether the job is simply a means to an end or whether it's the means itself that provides the feeling of fulfillment. Do you ever hear an artist grumbling that he *has* to go paint something or a musician whining that she *has* to go write down the tune that's been dancing through her head? Of course not! The true test of a creative calling such as art, music, or storytelling isn't in how much money you could make but, rather, would you still be drawn to it even if you never made a dime.

This was a disheartening revelation to an associate of mine several years ago. He had been laboring for some time over the opening chapter of his Great American Novel and clearly wasn't deriving much enjoyment from the exercise.

"So why are you doing it?" I asked.

"Because people who write novels make lots of money," he rationalized aloud. "Besides, all it takes is just one and then I'll be set for life."

Even if he should ever complete a first draft and actually submit it somewhere, he'll have yet to learn that the challenge of being a successful writer isn't about coming up with a single hot idea that will finance your entire future. It's about coming up with *multiple* ideas, one right after another, and being able to discern which among them are the most commercially viable to spend your time developing.

Like books, many people may well have just that one good script in them. For them, screenwriting is not a career but rather a labor of love to express one story, one time. The insights provided in this book will be useful in helping these people transform their great ideas into scripts that will get the attention of agents and directors. For the rest of you — those who want this as your full-fledged career and who constantly see the world around them as full of stories with compelling characters, high drama or low comedy — then start your journey here. Learn your craft well and appreciate the profound difference between what the eye *reads* and what the eye *sees*.

STRANGER IN A STRANGE LAND

The second thing to take into account is whether you're familiar enough with the medium to attempt to emulate it. In the workshops that I teach around the country and online, it never ceases to amaze me how many students are unversed in the very field that they want to write for. They are the wannabe playwrights who have never gone to the theater, the bright-eyed novelists who haven't read a book since back in high school, the aspiring screenwriters who never go to the movies. To use a travel analogy, they are the wayfarers who set off for a foreign country without learning the language, the currency, or the customs… and then wonder how they could possibly have gotten themselves so lost.

Nor do they avail themselves of the knowledge and advice of those who have gone before them. The volume of accessible interviews, Internet experts, and trade magazines leaves no excuse for haphazardly guessing the right way to develop, format, and pitch a story or, for that matter, to find out if that story has already been done.

Only last year, for example, a client approached me for coverage services on his script about a sweet-faced little alien who gets left behind by the mother ship and is befriended by a young boy.

"Sounds a lot like *E.T.*," I remarked.

"What's *E.T.*?" he asked.

Remember, if everyone could write a screenplay, screenwriters could not command such dear compensation for their invaluable creative talents. Similarly, while technology has expanded the realm of moviemaking to incredible dimensions, the basic formula for all movies, regardless of the genre, was cooked up decades ago. Learning about film from the many great film history books that can be found in bookstores or libraries is an invaluable first step in mastering the craft of screenwriting. There are no shortcuts in this business, so you might as well start at square one because, ultimately, you'll have to go there anyway.

WE REALLY LOVE IT, BUT….

The third requirement to be a working screenwriter is an extraordinarily thick skin to deal with rejection. Given the expense of making and distributing a feature film in today's economy, producers have more reasons to say "no" to you than to hand you a standard rich-and-famous contract for your efforts. Even the front-line script readers who make the determination to recommend or pass on your submission aren't picking the latter just to be mean-spirited twits; they only want to hang on to their jobs.

The bottom line is that no one along the industry food chain wants to be the one responsible for giving the greenlight to certifiable turkeys like *Ishtar, Heaven's Gate*, and *Gigli*. Accordingly, they prefer to err on the side of caution.

Even if your project *does* get optioned for development, there's absolutely no assurance that what will eventually end up on the screen will bear any resemblance to what initially came out of your printer. Screenwriting is all about rewriting, rewriting, and then rewriting some more.

I am reminded of an editor who once gushed and glowed about a fiction manuscript I had submitted to her. "It's perfect," she said. "It just needs some fix-up between pages 5 and 389." Since the total novel was only 400 pages, I was understandably puzzled as to which parts, exactly, had garnered the praise of perfection.

What you need to remember is that the incessant tweaking isn't designed to diminish your control but rather to maximize the story's appeal to target audiences. While there's nothing wrong with defending your creative vision it, nonetheless, carries the risk of either a second screenwriter being brought in to take over or the entire project being shelved for "artistic differences."

A case in point is *The Spellbox*, a Scottish time travel screenplay which I adapted from one of my published novels. As of this writing, the script currently is being re-engineered to accommodate the casting of younger leads. "The investors love it," my producer said, "but they'd really like Lucy and Max to be twentysomethings."

My initial reaction was one of protest. The characters, after all, were fashioned after a friend and myself, two worldly women who haven't been twentysomethings for —um, awhile. Fortunately, I confined my protesting to my husband, who fills the crucial role of major brainstormer and moral barometer. "Audiences like to see characters they can relate to," he pointed out. Since the fish-out-of-water plot still remained intact, the actual age of the leads wasn't that critical. While he agreed with me that he liked the maturity of Lucy and Max as originally written in the book, the alternative of fighting the issue also might have required me to give the money back.

It's hard to argue with such well-grounded logic. The point is that there are many very successful screenwriters whose works bear very little relationship to what is ultimately produced. While a literary work is generally a collaborative effort between an author and an editor, a produced film involves many people, the screenwriter, producer, director, actors, and, in many cases, additional screenwriters.

Your script can run the gamut from a completed painting to a penciled outline waiting for others to add the color, depth, and pathos necessary to transfer it from the printed page to the silver screen. Understanding your role in this competitive and creative process is vital if you are to master this craft.

WHAT MAKES AN IDEA 'CATCHY?'

If you want to write for the movies or television, you need to have an understanding of not only what makes for a catchy plot but also what constitutes a "filmable" concept.

"Catchy" equates to what the industry calls "high-concept." Essentially, high-concept ideas can be distilled into one defining sentence that tells you everything you need to know.

For example:

> A shipwrecked couple with three sons improvises on a tropical island. *Swiss Family Robinson*

> An abused wife fakes her own death in order to escape her abusive environment. *Sleeping With The Enemy*

> A losing baseball team is turned around by some divine intervention. *Angels In The Outfield*

> An orphaned baby is raised by gorillas. *Tarzan*

> A computer operator inadvertently receives a British agent's SOS. *Jumpin' Jack Flash*

> A coma victim's family mistakenly assumes that the woman who saved his life is his fiancee. *While You Were Sleeping*

These mini-summations are then spun by the marketing departments into movie posters, promotions, and billboards. As you start to develop your own film idea, imagine what it would look like if you saw it advertised in the Sunday movie section of your local paper. Could you sum up its premise in just one sentence *and* make viewers want to go see it?

"Filmable" relates to the constraints of time, technology, and budget but also applies to whether the storyline is primarily driven by action, dialogue, or imagination. (We'll get into this in greater detail in the next chapter on stage, page, or cinema.)

Several years ago, when I served on the board of directors of a local access station, I was asked to judge a 10-minute script contest whereby selected winners would have three days to shoot their films locally, using the studio's equipment. One particularly ambitious entrant turned in an apocalyptic drama in which 4,000 Imperial stormtroopers chase Elvis across the Tower Bridge just before the entire thing explodes into a fiery inferno.

Even if the script had been brilliantly written (which it seriously wasn't), it was encumbered by elements that far exceeded time, space, and available resources. This is an important consideration to keep in mind if you're pitching your project to independent producers with lots of heart but limited capital. In theory, they may love your storyline but need to pass on it because it would be impossible for them to do it justice.

It's critical to remember that this is a medium in which the most unique vision and storytelling approach must still conform to a standardized format. Your boundary-breaking plot must still resonate with the fundamental value system of the audience who will watch it. The thousands of films made every year throughout the world display a kaleidoscope of universes, themes, environments, characters, and relationships, but while you have all the colors you can imagine to create your script, you still have to color within a well-defined set of lines of format, plot, character development, and dialogue.

SIZZLE, STEAK, OR THE BEST OF BOTH?

Plots that rely heavily on special effects would seem to be a natural for the big screen. Even before the advent of CGI technology (computer generated imagery), producers were employing stop-action photography, miniaturized sets, and built-to-scale models to recreate primeval worlds, pirate battles on the open sea, and even King Kong taking swipes at airplanes from atop the Empire State Building.

While movies have become more visually stimulating, however, it often has been at the expense of plot and character. *Pearl Harbor*, for instance, had all the requisite you-are-there sight and sound explosions to simulate the horror of December 7, 1941, but fell short in delivering an empathetic love story that was compelling enough to justify its price tag and media hype.

Contrast this to 1965's *In Harm's Way*, in which the World War II Pacific theater battle scenes are pretty hokey by today's standards but the character nuances, sexual tension, and dialogue still make it a watchable film.

Consider, as well, the original *Star Wars* released in 1977 versus any of its eye-popping 'prequels' about the life and times of Darth Vader. Somewhere in the passage of 25 years, the emphasis shifted from characters whom audiences could genuinely cheer (or hiss) about to an ensemble that largely wanders around as talking props against a high-tech backdrop.

As I always advise my students and clients, if you can strip away all the glitz and gizmos and your story still has something substantive to say to an audience, you've probably got yourself a solid plot. If, however, the glitz and gizmos are *needed* to hold your viewers' attention, be forewarned that no amount of money in the world can save a limp plot from going straight to Lodge.net and the bargain video bin within the first month of opening.

SO WHAT *DOES* YOUR STORY HAVE TO SAY?

You may not have given it much thought before now but every movie — no matter how wacky, heart-tugging, disturbing, or far-fetched — has an underlying message or philosophy that it means to leave with us by the final credits.
For instance:

> > Love conquers all.
> > Appearances are deceiving.
> > Friends are just strangers we haven't met yet.
> > Love is blind.
> > Honesty is the best policy.
> > There's no place like home.

Arising from the film's message is the antithesis statement — the conflict which drives the action forward.

If, for instance, you want to demonstrate that true love has the power to vanquish all obstacles, the plot needs to be "obstacle-intensive" in order to present a significant-enough threat to the protagonist's romantic future. Or let's say that your storyline sets out to prove that there's no place like home. Accordingly, the alternatives to the homefront have to contest the latter's shortcomings in such a way as to make them seem inferior choices for the long-term.

Both the message and anti-message require that the lead characters' motivations be driven by one or more of the three core themes of fiction: reward, revenge, and escape. There has to be something major at stake for which they will risk whatever they have in order to win it (i.e., romance, riches, recognition), to get even with it (i.e., annihilation, retaliation, humiliation), or just to get away from it (i.e., prison, paranormal, political oppression). All action, thus, is an instrument of resolution, pointing up the need to stay focused on what your characters have to accomplish by the movie's end.

In order to understand how this principle works, consider each of the following films and identify which themes are prevalent:
> *Braveheart*
> *Thelma And Louise*
> *Galaxy Quest*
> *Tootsie*
> *Casablanca*
> *The Quiet Man*
> *Carrie*
> *Overboard*

HOW TO SAY IT AND FOR HOW LONG
Once you decide what your movie message and theme are going to be, you'll need to determine its genre and ideal length. Just as a catchy melody can be played in any number of different tempos (march, waltz, swing, etc.), so, too, can a catchy plot be orchestrated in a variety of genres and evoke different responses from audiences. The challenge is in determining which genre best captures the mood of the story you want to tell.

One of my journalism professors in college had a fondness for pop quizzes involving the composition of spontaneous news stories. From start to finish, we had exactly 10 minutes to come up with something that was both credible and entertaining. "Always go with your first instinct," he advised. "It will usually be your best lead." The students who ignored this, of course, were always the ones wearing deer-in-the-headlights panic at 9-1/2 minutes because they were convinced their first thoughts weren't good enough for development.

The same practice applies to deciding what genre best fits your idea for a movie.

Take into account what your reaction was when the idea first came to you. Was it an incident that made you double up with laughter? Was it a headline that made you gasp in shock and want to hug your children? Was it a dark and stormy night that made you steal uneasy glances over your shoulder? Whatever your reaction is/was to the event that gave you inspiration should be your first choice. That's not to say you can't change your mind as the storyline develops, but it gives you a starting point.

What's that, you say? Your plot involves Wild West era lovers who time-travel to Pluto and get involved in a musical-comedy-paranormal-murder investigation?

Unfortunately, Hollywood doesn't recognize the western/romance/sci-fi/musical/comedy/thriller category as a viable market. While it's certainly true that a number of movies incorporate *elements* of multiple genres, they are generally compartmentalized as one of the following for the convenience of industry PR, screenwriting competitions, and, of course, retailers who need to know where exactly to place them on the shelves and in the video catalogues:

> Comedy
> Drama
> Action
> Horror
> Romance
> Romantic Comedy
> Spoof/Satire
> Historical/Biographical
> Science Fiction
> Time Travel
> Thriller/Suspense
> Western
> Fantasy/Supernatural
> Musical
> Mystery
> Film Noir

The choice of genre has a direct bearing on the character development, the language used, the number of locations, and the overall pace of the script. So, too, does the projected length of the story. Is it essentially a one-joke scenario that can be conveyed in a 10-30 minute short? Or is it a multi-layered plot that needs a full two hours?

As a recent example, I was in the grocery store one afternoon when I overheard a young man panic to his buddy that he had just spied an ex-girlfriend at the check-stand just two lines over. He clearly didn't want to be seen by her. Was he upset because (1) he didn't want to provoke an emotional scene, (2) he was embarrassed by his sloppy appearance, (3) he had broken up with her on the false premise that his company was transferring him overseas, or (4) he was in the witness protection program and she was the reason why?

A humorous re-enactment of this situation would result in a completely different "feel" than a dark one whereby this chance encounter could unleash a chain of violence involving innocent bystanders. The genre choice would then influence whether the material could be contained within the boundaries of a snappy comedy sketch or require a more lengthy and detailed exposition of the ex-couple's relationship utilizing flashbacks.

Given my long-standing affinity for the funny, I opted for a 20-minute stage comedy entitled *Reversals Of Fortune* (Plays, Inc., Publishers). In this version, the young man was a bag-boy whose former love had dumped him in favor of the wealthy employer for whom they both worked. His discomfiture at being seen in such a lowly job is assuaged when he discovers that not only did *she* get subsequently dumped and lose her job but is now paying for her purchases with food stamps.

LAST BUT NOT LEAST, FOR WHOM, EXACTLY, ARE YOU WRITING THIS?

To whom do you think your movie idea would most appeal? Teenage boys? Middle-aged women? Families? Senior citizens? In order for your film to tug at all the right emotional chords, it helps to understand what issues are on the front burner for your target viewers.

With teens, for instance, angst and identity are tied into plots about coming of age, breaking rules, and spreading wings. Middle-aged women are a core market for romance, whether it relates to finding a new one or surviving the break-up of an old one.

Families are drawn to films that not only bring all of them together for a night out but espouse values and morality benchmarks that will continue to keep alive a deep and abiding respect for each other, long after the show itself is over. Older moviegoers are drawn to films that celebrate the best of the past, reinforcing a clarity of purpose and integrity they deem to be darkly elusive in the present. Themes of reunion and redemption are also especially strong.

Most of all, examine the kind of films that *you*, as a film fan, personally enjoy watching. For writing isn't just an exercise in writing about what you *know*; it's also in writing about what you really *like*!

GETTING STARTED

Buy yourself an idea book for recording potential plots, character sketches, and, yes, even titles and snippets of dialogue. It can either be a blank journal, a spiral bound tablet, or even a mini-notebook that you can tuck into your purse, brief-case, or glove compartment. The main thing is that it be easily accessible for you to jot down your thoughts before they get away!

For each idea you come up with, make a brief notation of the following:

1. SOURCE | If it were derived from something already existing (i.e., a book, a newspaper item, an interview), you'll need to explore the legalities of optioning or adapting the material to fit your particular inspiration. If it was a completely original thought, keep in mind how hard it is to maintain enthusiasm and momentum for a project once the initial

euphoria wears off. By being able to remind yourself of what you were doing when the thought first struck, you can reinvigorate yourself to keep working on it and see it through to completion.

2. MESSAGE | What does your idea have to say about the human condition, the fickleness of fate, the cyclical nature of history, etc.? If you haven't glanced at any books on proverbs lately, this could be a good time to do so. Proverbs are a helpful way to crystallize your concept and give you something to refer to whenever you feel as if you're getting off track.

3. THEME | What motivates your characters? Is it reward, revenge, escape, or a combination of the three? If they're not motivated by much of anything, you probably also don't have much of a story, either.

4. BEST GENRE FOR THIS STORY | While you're at it, list two other possible genres, as well. Down the road, when you've written yourself into a mental cul-de-sac, this could come in handy.

5. TARGET AUDIENCE | Who, besides your immediate family and friends, would find this story as compelling as you do? Why?

CHAPTER 2 | STAGE, PAGE, OR CINEMA?

We generally don't think of the bigger-than-life canvas of moviemaking as having any limitations whatsoever when, in fact, it really does. Knowledge of what a film can and can't accomplish within its parameters and bank account is what could spell the difference between exploring and successfully selling your concept to another medium or accruing a string of rejections by keeping it "as is."

As you read through this chapter, try to imagine which elements have the most bearing on your film idea(s) as well as what degree of intimacy and lasting memory you would like to create with the audience for which each plot is written.

THE ELEMENT OF TIME

To begin with, you have two hours (or less) of screen-time to tell your entire story to a captive audience. Unlike a theater script, which also runs about two hours, the story is delivered straight through, without any intermissions. Unlike playwrights, whose medium provides a printed program to clue the audience in on relationships and time/space transitions, screenwriters need to impart these same details through dialogue, title cards, physical changes in character appearance, and cinematography (i.e., dissolves, dream sequences, split screens, etc.).

Because of the relatively short timeframe of both films and stage plays, there isn't a lot of room for pleasantly meandering backstory and leisurely exposition. We are, instead, the vicarious witnesses to an inciting incident or interaction which will impact the main characters' lives in ways which they had not anticipated. We all know that they were doing *something* prior to FADE IN and AT RISE but our primary concern is (1) what are they all doing as of right now and (2) why we should care about the outcome.

Long-term bedfellows Alan Alda and Ellen Burstyn in the screen adaptation of Bernard Slade's play, Same Time, Next Year. *(Mirisch Corporation/Universal Studios, 1978). Unlike most adaptations which expand the cast and number of locations, this film closely parallels Slade's original two-person stage comedy. The passage of time is depicted not only through costumes and makeup but through the use of news headlines and photos between each vignette of George and Doris' relationship.*

Contrast the physical pacing of these mediums to a novel, the average length of which is 350 pages. Unlike movies and plays, the duration it takes to absorb a book's message is completely removed from the author's control, depending on consumers' reading skills, interest level in the subject matter, and availability of free time.

Since the written word can also cover more historical, geographical, physical, emotional, and spiritual ground than either a movie or play, novelists have more freedom to incorporate subplots, juxtapose personal commentary, or — ala Michener — start the story out with pterodactyls and gradually introduce humans around page 605.

SELF-TEST

> Do you feel that you can comfortably tell your entire story in two hours or less?
> If not, what elements in this story would require a longer time-frame to convey?
> Are these elements essential to the audience's understanding of the storyline and character motivations? If so, what other components of the story would you be willing to delete in order to keep those in?
> Which of the three mediums — movies, plays, or books — do you personally enjoy the most? Why?

LOCATION, LOCATION, LOCATION

Movies and books share the advantage of not only being able to travel forward and backward but globe-trot faster than the Concorde. In one scene or chapter, we're dining on the Riviera; in the very next, we can be wielding machetes in the jungles of Bolivia. Books, of course, have an economic edge in that regard; specifically, it costs exactly the same to print a page that transpires in 17th century Austria as it does to print one that all takes place in your grandmother's attic.

For that reason, a book publisher probably will be more amenable to buying your multi-location tome than a producer will be to opening his or her wallet for a newcomer's screenplay that utilizes an equal number of locales. On a more insular level, producers look critically at how many times the camera is moved just within the context of one primary location; i.e., a house, a school, an office building.

While film is a visual medium that needs to keep our attention riveted on the screen, to flip your characters from one backdrop to another without any real reason for doing so will not only add to the production budget but add to the amount of set up and strike down time involved in moving the cameras, lights, sound systems, etc.

Stage plays are even more difficult — though not impossible — when it comes to accommodating multiple locations. One of the built-in advantages, of course, is that the spectators are already aware that their imaginations will be called upon to fill in the level of detail that the physical staging area precludes from actually being constructed for them.

We can simply *tell* them that a given scene is taking place in the dungeon of a Scottish castle and they will believe it without our having to erect the entire castle above it, bring livestock into the courtyard, or even fill a murky moat. We don't even need to show archers on the parapets to suggest that this realm is well protected, for it can be conveyed with as little as a single line of dialogue exchanged between the characters.

Although extravagant Broadway productions have hydraulic lifts, turntables, holograms, and all manner of techno-toys at their disposal to convey multiple venues and dimensions of time, it's nonetheless amazing what even the most modest community theater can do with lighting, platforms, blackouts, and min-imalist set design.

SELF-TEST

> How many locations do you need to effectively convey your film idea?
> How many of them require specific representation (i.e., down-town San Francisco)?
> How many of them could go the generic route (i.e., large city)?
> How many of them are completely incidental to what is being communicated by the actors through dialogue and action?
> Is each location appropriate to the mood and pace you want to convey?
> How many of your locations are cliché? (i.e., characters being introspective on airplanes; mother/daughter confrontations in the kitchen.)

DEGREE OF INTIMACY

It's hard to feel really in touch with movie characters when you're staring up at 15-foot-high faces and listening to them speak to each other in Surround-Sound. Likewise, the media hype and saturation never let us stray very far from the fact that the names of the actors and actresses are what we are programmed to remember more so than the names of any of the characters they happen to be playing.

What this translates to in terms of intimacy is a transitory moment whereby the suspension of disbelief centers more on how the role is acted rather than how the plot is intended to affect us on an interpersonal level. By the time it takes us to warm up to Meryl Streep's latest accent or believe in Brendon Frasier as an Indiana Jones-style adventurer (*The Mummy*), we're already a quarter or more of the way into the story.

Contrast this to books that instantly engage us by allowing us to do our own casting or stage plays which invite us to relate to characters who are relatively our same size and not over-amped by microphones and speakers. The challenge to writers in either of these two mediums is the creation of personas whose consistency can withstand the test of time and whose psychological makeup is open to the demands of diverse interpretations.

The performance nature of plays, for instance, requires tightly drawn characters whose presence is capable of absorbing and superseding the identity of the actors themselves, no matter how famous their reputations. I'm reminded of having had the privilege of seeing Richard Burton in one of his last performances of *Camelot*. Hard an act as this compelling man would be to follow, it is the essence of vulnerability captured in the character of Arthur, himself, as a young husband, friend, and king that leaves the door open for successive actors to play the same role and not be judged as lesser.

These differences will be important to keep in mind when you start developing your ideas. The more emotional connectivity you would like to establish between your characters and a prospective audience, the more intimate their introductory delivery platform needs to be.

Genre plots, in which the central conflict derives from an external base, generally lend themselves well to film, while internal, character-driven conflicts yield more audience connection in print and on-stage, owing to more personal frames of reference and the time to process information at higher levels of abstraction.

SELF-TEST
> Is your central conflict primarily driven by external or internal forces?
> Is it more important to you that your main characters be remembered for themselves or for the celebrities who portrayed them?

THE ROAR OF THE CROWD

If your movie idea calls for swarms of humanity, films and novels are your best bet for containing them. Again, of course, you're looking at escalating budget concerns the higher the number of bodies you need to evoke the requisite realism for your epic.

Books, of course, can manage this challenge quite easily. Bring on the Cavalry! Bring on the Huns! Bring on the hordes of after-Thanksgiving Day shoppers! On paper, you can have as big a stampede as you want and it won't cost you a penny extra.

Movies are dealing more and more with crowd management through the innovations of CGI (computer generated imagery), although they still need to pay salaries, buy meals, provide costumes, dressing rooms, and workers' comp insurance for all of the real personas who comprise the cast and crew.

Also, you'd be surprised how many non-moving roles are portrayed nowadays by costumed mannequins. Take a close look, for instance, at the Santa Anita racetrack scenes in *Seabiscuit* and count how many of the spectators are actually plastic dummies wearing hats. For movies in which stuntperson costs are already exorbitant (i.e., *Titanic*), the problem is resolved with fabric dummies that can be temporarily tied to a pillar, post, or piece of furniture and break away easily as the air-borne result of an explosion, earthquake, ship-sinking, etc.

On stage, the size of the physical cast is dictated by the dimensions of the theater. Even if a large number of people were supposedly present at a designated event in the storyline, their presence is distilled, out of necessity, to a core handful. Theater audiences not only accept this downsizing but are also accepting of double-casting, the practice of assigning those characters in subordinate (and sometimes nameless) roles to appear in multiple parts.

A particularly stellar example of this is the musical version of *Titanic*, which opened in New York at roughly the same time James Cameron's version hit the movie theaters. In an innovative twist of staging, there are two sequential dining room scenes in which we see, respectively, the first class salon and steerage. Those dining in first class are accustomed to luxury and their enviable stations in life. Below decks, however, are the huddled masses who can't wait to start pursuing their dreams in this magical destination called America.

Listen carefully to the lyrics — and to the individual voices. You'll discover that they are being sung by the same actors — a device that not only utilizes a cast of several dozen to represent the ship's 2,000 passengers and crew, but poignantly illustrates just how thin the line is between the haves and have nots.

SELF-TEST
> How many people does it take to effectively tell your story?
> How many of them are expendable?
> Which characters will your audience most strongly relate to on
   a personal level?

AUTHOR INVOLVEMENT

Once your idea is written down and sold to someone, how much participation do you want to have in it thereafter? If you're someone who has a hard time letting go, this is a question you're really going to need to consider. Ironically, whether you say "yes" or "no" to being a further part of the development process, that decision is oftentimes vested with the buyer and not the seller.

As you'll see in the chapter on the realities of revision, it's rare for another person to love every word of your project exactly as much as you do and not want to change a single thing. In each of the three target markets we've been exploring, there are varying levels of author engagement. How you would respond to each scenario, of course, is dependent upon the underlying reason you wrote the book, play, or film to begin with.

For novelists (unless you go the self-publishing route), you'll be at the mercy of editors who want to tweak a character here and drop a paragraph there. While your idea has the strongest chance of staying intact if it's going to be released in print — as well as the fewest number of cooks interfering with the broth — it's nevertheless a one-shot venture. Just because you don't like the version that got released, you can't turn around and sell the same manuscript to a different publisher.

For theatrical works, your breadth of involvement in production is a factor of the rapport you've established with the director. Maybe you'll choose to go the workshop route, attending various staged readings and soliciting feedback from the cast and the audience members. Perhaps you'll even try your hand at directing the play yourself or entering a co-production arrangement with the resident director. Unlike books, of course, theater is an ever-evolving beast, courtesy of diversified casts and diversified audiences. Just because a show falls flat in Buffalo doesn't mean that it won't garner rave reviews in San Diego.

Screenplays — another one-shot venture — are subject to the most outside interference. If you don't believe that, just take a look at the list of credits at the end of any given film. More likely than not, your role in the process will end shortly after the ink has dried on the contract. Because the script's outcome is dependent on such a high number of variables, there simply isn't any way that your input as the original author could cover all the bases. What makes its way to the silver screen may, in fact, bear little resemblance to your own vision. It also may have a much shorter shelf-life than you hoped for, owing to the competitive bid for audience dollars and the proliferation of new films that come out every weekend.

What ultimately matters, however, is that — because of, or in spite of, your level of involvement — it still got made.

A ROSE BY ANY OTHER NAME
This is a favorite exercise I do with students in my workshops.

> Make a list of your 10 favorite movies.
> Scratch any movie off of this list that, to your knowledge, also exists as a stage play or as a novel.
> For whichever movies still remain on your list, identify whether or not they could effectively work as stage plays or as novels.
> Now take a look at your own movie idea. Could it work as a novel? Why or why not? Could it work as a stage play? Why or why not? Even though you may still come back to your original concept of developing it as a screenplay, this process enables you to view your plot from different perspectives and feel comfortable that you have chosen the best method of delivery.

CHAPTER 3 | PRE-EXISTING INSPIRATIONS

In the chapter on Page, Stage, or Cinema, we examined the characteristics of each as an aid to determining which medium would work best for your original idea. In this chapter, we'll look at the legal, structural, and interpretive components involved in adapting an existing work to a feature screenplay or short.

IN RETROSPECT

During the infancy of cinema, it's not surprising that the bulk of material was adapted from works that were originally written for the stage. The physical theatricality of melodramas and vaudeville skits didn't require sound in order for the plot to be understood. As title cards and onstage "ambiance" piano players gradually gave way to the first talkies, fledgling writers began to adapt more material from novels and short stories gleaned from magazines such as *Collier's* and the popular *Saturday Evening Post*.

During the 1960s and 1970s, adaptations of novels accounted for nearly a third of all movies produced in the United States. Today, that total has dropped to roughly 12% and is concentrated on power-house authors such as Michael Crichton, Tom Clancy, and that master of horror, Stephen King.

Novels and plays, however, haven't been the only sources of inspiration for screen material. Consider the following:

> Diaries and journals. The most famous of these, of course, was *The Diary of Anne Frank*.
> Comic strips. *Superman, Spider-Man, Dick Tracy...* need we say more?
> Games, both board and electronic. Examples: *Clue* and *Lara Croft, Tomb Raider*.

> Vintage photography. E. J. Bellocq's images of Storyville prosti-
tutes in 1917 Louisiana were the inspiration for Louis Malle's
Pretty Baby (1978).

> Psychological case studies. The demonically possessed girl in
The Exorcist was actually a boy in the real-life plot that came
to William Peter Blatty's attention.

> Details at 11. Pick any story that's made the day's headlines and
the odds are that it'll be a movie of the week within six
months.

While current statistics suggest that nearly 75% of current film fare is original, it doesn't take a rocket scientist to observe that the definition of "original" is murky at best. Do remakes of prior films such as *Sabrina* count as new? What about adaptations of foreign flicks; do translations and Americanized interpretations of their content constitute a fresh story or just a different spin? And where does one draw the originality line with *Star Trek* spoofs like *Galaxy Quest* or the similarities between Dorothy in *The Wizard Of Oz* and Luke Skywalker from *Star Wars*?

Inspiration comes in all shapes, sizes, and genres. It's how much of it you can claim as an original concept that makes the difference between a good day at the box office or a bad day in court.

IS IT YOURS FOR THE TAKING?

Let's say that it's three o'clock in the morning and you've just finished reading an absolutely breathtaking book. In your mind's eye, you already know whom you'd cast in the lead roles, what kinds of witty things they'd say to one another, and where you'd want to film it if it were a movie.

If it were a movie....

A light bulb clicks on your head. Why not write that script yourself? After all, you love the plot, you've bonded with the characters, and you even recognize — from reading this book — what it takes to deliver a visually compelling piece of cinema.

And hey, the author of the book—some woman in Great Britain named J.K. Rowling—might be so impressed that she'll write you a lovely thank you letter.

That's the fantasy.

The reality is that she'll have her attorney send you a not-so-lovely letter suing you for infringement of copyright.

It will take more than a wizard's magic to get you out of hot water and legal paperwork if you steal an idea that's not yours. (Harry Potter and the Sorcerer's Stone, *1492 Pictures/Heyday/Warner, 2001*)

Even if she had no desire whatsoever to turn Harry Potter and his adventures into a box-office blockbuster, it's illegal for you to steal the concept and turn it into something else. Just as you wouldn't want your own works "borrowed" by another writer, the rules of registration and copyright exist to protect those whose brilliance has preceded you. While that's not to say they wouldn't be flattered or even intrigued by your enthusiasm to reframe their masterpieces, you need to observe the proper protocol in acquiring permission.

Specifically, that procedure is:
> Find out whether the book, play, or short story is in the public
  domain.
> If the work is *not* in the public domain, determine what rights
  are available for option.
> Consult an attorney and get your agreement in writing.

When William Shakespeare wrote *Hamlet* or Louisa Mae Alcott wrote *Little Women*, neither one was concerned about someone coming along and turning their plots into movies. In the first place, movies hadn't been invented yet. Nor, for that matter, was there a regulatory agency to assign and monitor subsidiary rights.

Creative works that have fallen into what is called "public domain" are a gold mine for screenwriters who want to try their hand at modifying someone else's material. Specifically, the term applies to those works which were either published prior to 1923 or those which were published between 1923 and 1963 and were not renewed.

Today's copyright laws, by comparison, protect the work for the life of the author plus 70 years or until December 2047, whichever is greater. For collaborative works, this term is measured by whichever author lives longer. In addition, the United States has reciprocal copyright relations with most countries of the world.

Because public domain properties are no longer protected by copyright, they may be freely used by anyone who wants to do something with them. In addition to literary and performance art properties, public domain also applies to published works by the government and its agents and to autobiographical records and journals which have been granted or donated by their originator for the enlightenment of subsequent generations.

The ease with which you can ascertain who owns a particular copyright depends on the pivotal year 1978 and what part of the country you live in. Registrations, renewals, and copyright ownership transfers became available online from 1978 forward. Anything prior to that requires a manual record search of U.S. Copyright Office files.

If the Washington D.C. facility is within reasonable commuting distance — or if you're planning a working vacation to the nation's capital — you can do the search for free on your own. If, however, you need to press a staffer into service to do the looking for you, it will cost you approximately $75 per hour.

Additional information on this process is available through circulars published by the U.S. Copyright Office itself; specifically, Circular 22 ("How to Investigate the Copyright Status of a Work") and Circular 23 ("Copyright Card Catalog and the Online File"). Both can be ordered directly from the Web site at *www.copyright.gov*.

Issues covered include which rights have been granted as derivations of the original material; i.e., translations, radio, TV, film, Braille, etc. These are laid out at the time of the property's purchase, generally as a boilerplate clause for authors and their editors who don't have any immediate plans to spin the material into something different. The specific language regarding subsidiary venues has evolved in keeping with technology, public demand, and accessibility.

As recently as 10 years ago, for instance, no one had thought that the electronic medium would catch on as it did. That revolution resulted in a conundrum: could authors whose novels had been published traditionally reissue those works as "e-books" on the Internet — such extensions never were addressed in their original contracts. Nor had anyone predicted the proliferation of high-tech video games and merchandising associated with fantasy and science fiction stories.

What this means for aspiring screenwriters is a little sleuthing to determine which permissions can be granted to take a non-public domain plot to its next level.

The availability of film rights for existing books is contingent upon several factors. If, for instance, it was written by a well-established author and published by a major house, it's a pretty sure bet that a movie studio already has pounced on an option, if for no other reason than to keep someone else from doing it.

Even if film rights haven't been delineated at the time of publication, you still need to work through professional channels of corresponding with the publishing house and/or author's representative to ensure that they don't already have something in the works. In the case of deceased authors, heirs may have objections to strangers tweaking with their loved ones masterpieces in any way, shape, or form.

Smaller houses, foreign publishers, and self-published authors represent a better chance of negotiating permission for an adaptation because — in a nutshell — a film would (hopefully) promote and enhance the value of the original product. The downside, obviously, is that a prospective producer could argue, "If it hasn't set the house afire on its own merit, what makes you think people would go pay to see this at the movies?"

In the same vein, new plays that are produced in regional theaters or have their debuts on university stages are rich in opportunity for development. What many people don't realize is that these productions are often "shopped" a long time before officially finding a home with a publisher. The reason is threefold:

> The more times a script can be tested on an audience, the more chances to work all the bugs out before settling on a final version.

> Playwrights, such as myself, enjoy the freedom of being able to negotiate performance fees — and participate on the fringes as a consultant — for as long as possible.

> Major theatrical publishers such as Samuel French prefer to have proof of a show's popularity and longevity before making a commitment to aggressively market it.

In addition, the majority of aspiring playwrights tend not to have agents jumping into the mix, largely because agents view live theater as a riskier venture than books and, thus, one which offers a lot less return for their efforts. Playwrights also recognize, realistically, that film versions of their stories will have shorter shelf lives than the original plays and, accordingly, don't pose any long-term conflict of interest. Further, they're savvy enough to know that movie-goers outnumber theater aficionados and that movie adaptations will enable them to share their plots with people who otherwise would not have seen them at all.

So what happens after someone says "yes" to your proposal for an adaptation?

In a perfect world, promises could be sealed with a handshake or — in the case of e-mail — with a smiley face. Unfortunately, issues related to intellectual property rights require that both parties put signatures to it. This is when it comes in handy to have an entertainment law professional help you memorialize your option agreement.

In an option agreement, you essentially are "renting" the work for a specified amount of time and designating who gets what in the event of a sale. This protects your interests since the author can't turn around and cut a deal with a writer he or she likes better. The duration of this lease (usually 1-3 years) also protects the author from being saddled with a flake in the event the screenwriter procrastinates.

Do you want the original author to have a say-so in the finished product? If this is a concern, it needs to be addressed in the agreement. As a creative professional, the last thing you need is to pour all of your energy into a script, only to have the novelist or playwright come back and tell you to rewrite it. While input is always valuable in the adaptation process, it also can be a hindrance if the originators are either too wedded to their own words to allow others to orchestrate substitutions, or if they simply don't grasp what successful screenplays entail in terms of structure, pacing, and dynamics.

WHAT TO KEEP, WHAT TO LOSE

As someone who has done screenplay adaptations of books and stage plays, I can attest to the fact that it's a lot harder than it looks. The obsession to retain and compress as much of the original source material as possible into a smaller box makes you lose sight of what you're trying to accomplish; specifically, to relate the story on a different level.

Just because you have to whittle a 500-page tome down to a 98-page screenplay doesn't mean that those 402 pages of literary brilliance will never be appreciated. As long as the book itself remains in print, all those fabulous words and extraneous scenes you had to painfully delete for the medium of film will still be available.

Novels and theater scripts hold opposite challenges when it comes to the adaptation process.

For novels, it's obviously a matter of excessive verbiage. Historical narrative, detailed descriptions, bridging passages, character thought-bubbles, anecdotal pauses, retrospective commentary, etc., have to be sacrificed in the interest of keeping momentum and staying focused on the central conflict.

Non-fiction texts — the fodder of many a documentary — call for their own brand of selective editing. On the one hand, verbatim passages can be pasted into the script because the majority of lines are straight narration, not chatty conversation. On the other hand, the whole thing needs to be stitched together with the appropriate visuals, interviews, and relevance to contemporary viewers. And, because they are spun from a fact-based orientation rather than a fictional one, adaptations of this nature are generally deemed more educational or inspirational than they are entertaining.

Budgetary considerations factor into the equation, too. While it's the same cost to print a book page that describes 10,000 Chinese warriors running across The Great Wall as it is to describe a single guy eating dinner in a Chinese restaurant, it's a lot cheaper to film the latter.

Although you certainly never want to let pesky details like money put a rein on your muse, if you're planning to pitch your script to a studio with modest means, you need to develop an eye for what's a necessity and what's a frill. This sense of prudence applies to supplemental characters as well, forcing you to downsize the book's original population to those who have a clear-cut reason for existing in the plot.

Dialogue in a book-to-film adaptation also needs to be significantly restructured to take into account the fact that conversations written to be *read* tend to be more formal and articulate than those which are written to be *spoken*. Book characters, for instance, use less slang, interrupt each other less often, speak in longer sentences, and put together sound combinations that would be awkward if they had to be delivered out loud; i.e., "Sheila sells soft-shelled seashells, doesn't she?"

While dialogue is clearly less of a problem with stage-to-film conversions, the onus on the writer is to figure out how to expand the story beyond the borders of the living room, bedroom, or front porch where the theatrical plot transpires. As of this writing, I am involved in such a dilemma with the adaptation of *Muriel's Memoirs*, one of my two-act dramas, to a feature-length film. The producer wants to keep the story to the cast of four women and yet move them out into the community, incorporate flashbacks, and go into greater depth on the influences that shaped their respective personalities.

The larger problem, however, is in figuring out how to introduce "visual stimulation" in a storyline where the characters do more sitting and talking than getting up and running around. To this end, I rely on my library of videos to appreciate how others have handled this question. If, indeed, adaptation is a route that you want to go in your screenwriting career, familiarizing yourself with what filmmakers consider to be watchable elements is a tremendous aid in deciding what can be eliminated and what needs to be elaborated.

 In the stage version of *Steel Magnolias*, for example, all of the action takes place in Truvy's beauty salon. We accept the static nature of the stage set because we're more interested in getting to know the owner, her assistant, and the four women who frequent her shop. While the film adaptation is still about the bond of friendship that exists among these women, even the talents of an all-star cast could not hold our attention if the camera never moved beyond the sinks and the hairdryers.

The Lion In Winter (1968), is an excellent comparison piece as well, allowing us to move throughout Henry and Eleanor's castle and even outdoors rather than confining the royal family's struggle for power to one central room. Historical pieces such as this also invite comparison to their counterparts in print, in which a plethora of dates, places, battles, and so forth are only sparingly referenced in the course of natural dialogue.

LOST IN TRANSLATION

No two people are going to read a book, watch a play, or see a movie and get exactly the same thing out of it. Likewise, whatever personal inspiration you derive from a work you want to adapt to a screenplay may not be what the original author intended at all. Criticisms such as, "She just doesn't get it," "He completely left out the second sister," and "Why did they go and change the ending?" are common reactions among consumers who expect adaptations to be carbon copies of the original material. The inability to accept that it's just one person's viewpoint inhibits them from appreciating that "different" can sometimes translate to "better."

I recall the great lengths to which one of my literature professors would go in analyzing Nathaniel Hawthorne's *The Scarlet Letter*. She adamantly "tsk-tsked" what was then (1979) an upcoming television mini-series starring Meg Foster.

"Mr. Hawthorne," she archly declared, "would roll over in his grave."

Goodness knows, of course, what she opined to her students 16 years later when Hawthorne's heroine was resurrected yet again, this time by an actress who posed au natural on the cover of a national magazine.

With no way of knowing what Hawthorne's mindset was when he first wrote it, we obviously have no way of accurately guessing his reaction to any of the adaptations. Was he deeply wedded to the pain and humiliation of the star-crossed lovers? Or did its completion represent nothing more than a chunk of change with which to pay his mortgage on a house with seven gables?

Keep that in mind as you struggle with the riddle of the "right" way to communicate someone else's story.

LEARNING BY EXAMPLE

The following interview with screenwriter John Collee first appeared in the November/December 2003 issue of *Screentalk* and is included here with the magazine's gracious permission. Collee's insights on developing a single film from an existing book series will be of benefit to anyone intrigued by the adaptation process.

Master and Commander:
The Far Side of the World

I must down to the seas again,
To the lonely sea and the sky,
And all I ask is a tall ship
And a star to steer her by.
And the wheel's kick and the wind's song
And the white sail's shaking,
And a gray mist on the sea's face
And a gray dawn breaking.

John Masefield
Sea Fever (1902)

In centuries past, the open sea was a welcome refuge for young men seeking adventure, for criminals escaping the gallows, and for bachelors dodging matrimony. In more recent times, its mesmerizing power could be experienced vicariously in swashbuckling films such as *Captain Blood*, *The Black Swan*, *Captain Horatio Hornblower* and *Crimson Pirate*.

Just in time for the 2003 holiday season, novelist Patrick O'Brian's seafaring series, *Master and Commander*, set sail on movie screens across the country. Under the direction of Peter Weir and starring Russell Crowe as Captain Jack Aubrey, the script was adapted from O'Brian's 10th book, *The Far Side of the World*, by screenwriter John Collee.

Collee, who trained as a doctor in Edinburgh, Scotland, is no stranger to globe-trotting adventures himself, having worked in Africa, the Far East, the former Soviet Union, and the Pacific, often writing about his experiences in a weekly newspaper column which ran for six years in the U.K.'s Observer Newspaper. He took time from his busy schedule to offer insights on the challenges of adapting an 1800s era war story to a movie that could resonate with modern audiences.

Patrick O'Brian was a prolific writer and Captain Aubrey had no shortage of adventures during the early 19th century. When writing this screenplay, was there some consideration given to the notion that this may be one of several movies based upon the same characters?
As far as I know, Fox owns the rights to all the novels so, as you say, there's bags of material for a sequel. However, preparing the ground for that was never part of the brief. We set out to write a movie which was satisfying and complete in its own right. It always seemed unlikely to me that we'd be lucky enough to get Peter Weir and Russell Crowe for more than one movie.

What particular problems are created for you as a screenwriter if, in a sequel or additional movie with the same characters, there are different actors playing the lead roles? For example, it is hard to imagine anyone other than Harrison Ford playing Indiana Jones. Ford, however, was one of three actors

to play Jack Ryan in adaptations of Tom Clancy's novels. Does an adaptation of a novel make this less of a problem because, over the years, the readers have developed their own relationships with the character rather than — in the *Indiana Jones* series — people being introduced to a serial character through the medium of film?

I try not to think of any specific actor in the role I'm writing (or in this case co-writing). You have to take the characters from your imagination or from the novel you're adapting and render them as faithfully as possible. If the characters are well-realized and consistent, I suppose any actors can then take the roles and make them theirs.

The premise of the O'Brian series revolves around the relationship between Captain Aubrey and his surgeon friend, Stephen Maturin, a Napoleonic-era secret agent. To what do you attribute the popularity and longevity of these books? (Author note: O'Brian died in January 2000 at the age of 85.)

Finely observed characters. A world you can entirely immerse yourself in, full of strange curiosities. A canvas as big as the world's oceans but as small and intimate as the enclosed wooden world of a ship. A history lesson with an intriguing, never-ending narrative all its own. Stories which, despite their foreign and exotic settings, confront issues that are contemporary in nature and, indeed, timeless: Is there a "just" war? Is patriotism good or bad? Does power corrupt? When are principles more important than friendship?

Is there a particular reason why *The Far Side of the World* was adapted rather than any other in the series as one that would resonate with 21st century audiences?

All of O'Brian's plots tend to meander a great deal. As a novelist, he goes where the feeling takes him, which is not a luxury you can afford on film. However, this book is more focused than most: our heroes chase a pirate ship from the Pacific into the Atlantic and the journey, with all of its trials, tests a lifelong friendship between the ship's captain, Jack, and her doctor, Stephen. Peter and I took that simple idea and developed our own variation of the plot, jettisoning several elements from what originally existed in *The Far Side of the World* and replacing them with episodes from some of the other O'Brian novels.

When doing an adaptation of a historical novel, are you more or less concerned about historical accuracy than you would be if you were writing a stand-alone screenplay set in another era?
I'm concerned to make it accurate whether it's my own work or somebody else's. In other historical adaptations I've taken on, I invariably start by buying a ton of second-hand books on the Internet — anything that I can read about similar people in a similar time — which might help me inhabit the world of the story as fully as the novelist did. This is one project where that wasn't necessary. O'Brian had written so much about shipboard life in and around 1812, that all you had to do was read his novels.

When doing an adaptation such as this, do you find it easier to (1) take outline notes throughout the reading of the original text or (2) read the text, then rely on your memory to conjure forth those scenes that were the most lasting?
I scribble on books a lot. In a complicated book I'll mark up what's happening in the margin of each page so I can flip through and find sections I'm looking for. *The Season of the Jew*, which I adapted recently for Working Title/Roger Donaldson, was some 600 pages long with a very tortuous plot. I wrote myself an exact synopsis of the book - some 200 sequences, then whittled this down to the 30 of 40 sequences which constituted the film. In linear stories like *The Season of the Jew* this is fairly simple. In complex, multicharacter plots it's sometimes a useful exercise to write out each character strand separately and then interweave them.

I know what you mean about reading and then free-associating from memory; it can really help. To go a step further, actually "talking" the story is an invaluable way of sorting out the tangle. When you're telling a tale verbally you automatically condense the boring bits and extend the suspenseful part, depending on the listener's reaction.

You can't introduce too many characters too soon or your listener gets muddled, so it forces you to pace the story sensibly and to put in backstory only when it's necessary. If you're "performing" — as in a pitch — the adrenaline rush really stimulates creativity. With *Sixteen Pleasures*, which I adapted recently from the Robert Hellenga novel for Handprint and Nicole Kidman, I internalized the story, then told it in my own words over and over again to various prospective financiers. The initial 10-minute pitch became a 40-minute pitch, which eventually became the script.

With *Master and Commander*, Peter Weir and I used all the above techniques. We read and annotated the central book (*The Far Side of the World*). We wrote out plot points on cards and shuffled them on a cork board until the story was working. I'd then write out each sequence in my own words and relate it to Peter each morning. As the story progressed, he'd scribble on these sequences, amend and edit, add and discard. Finally we had a 50-page prose document which read as the film and that was what the first draft script was based on.

When does the dialogue start to kick in?
I try not to add dialogue till the very end, when I know exactly what each sequence has to achieve. It's so easy to get locked into neat dialogue that doesn't serve the script.

What happens when you hit mental speedbumps?
When a draft isn't working I always go back to synopsis form. Write the story out in prose again, repair the plot, then rewrite the script to that pattern. It's hopeless to try and fiddle with a 120-page script without reducing it in this way to a manageable narrative.

Had the author of the *Master and Commander* series still been alive to consult when you began work on the screenplay, would you have found his active participation in the screenwriting process to be a help or a hindrance?
As an author I'm all for it because they know so much about the world of the story and the inner lives of their characters. As you know, the best adaptations

are often quite dissimilar in structure to the novel but novelists, like screenwriters, are generally fascinated by the mechanism of story and only too happy to unpick and reconfigure their work. I'm sure O'Brien would have been into it. Peter and I often talked of how we wished he was physically present at our meetings. It often seemed that he was there in spirit.

Given the world events over the past few years, do you think the public will respond to the movie differently now than if you had penned it earlier?
It's essentially a pirate movie. You know who the good guys are. People are nostalgic for that kind of moral clarity, especially nowadays. It's also about people who lived in an era when suffering and death were commonplace. Nineteenth century sailors accepted a level of risk and daily tragedy which most of us would find intolerable. But it was normal to them. Mostly they ignored all the bad stuff that could happen and got on with their lives. That spirit of cheerful perseverance is something we in the West need to re-learn. Now more than ever.

What problems would you have envisioned as a screenwriter if the film had been based on the novel's premise of an enemy American warship during the War of 1812 rather than a French warship during the Napoleonic Wars?
Financial problems (for myself and for the movie). The primary market for this film is North America. Making Americans the bad guys would not have been good for box office! For 95% of the film, anyway, the enemy ship is a cipher — a ghost they are chasing into the unknown. The nationality of its crewmen is kind of irrelevant.

When writing a movie whose underlying theme is war, do you try to focus on resolution of that underlying conflict or do you focus on the effects of that conflict upon the people so engaged? If the latter, does that also change the nature of the characters who represent the enemy in this conflict and, if so, how? For instance, do you make the French equally honorable and somewhat sympathetic or do you make them even more vile in order to evoke a strong emotional response in the audience for the heroes?
You write about the effects of the conflict on the characters, anything else is liable to be polemical. *Master and Commander* is one of those war films like *Platoon*,

or *Das Boot* where the enemy is largely invisible. You see the whole conflict from one side (The Americans in *Platoon*, the Germans in *Das Boot*, The Brits in *Master and Commander*), but every character has a slightly different view on not only how to prosecute this war but also on the rights and wrongs of the conflict — and that's where the real drama comes from.

How long did it take you to write *Master and Commander*?
It was a couple of years from first meeting to start of filming. Not all of that was spent writing, of course. The first draft took three or four months, then we showed it to the studio and got feedback. The other drafts took progressively less time, but they continued until we started shooting.

How many rewrites did you go through?
Peter and I did many drafts of the synopsis, then four or five complete drafts of the script. There were rewrites to get the story right and rewrites to get the budget down and a couple of radical changes such as when we decided that the sole woman on board was skewing the plot and would have to go. On one draft we lost 30 pages off the opening. On another draft we totally reconceived that last act.

Do you prefer adaptations or scripting an original story from scratch?
I like writing fiction. I'm less keen on dramatizations of real life events where you're limited by your obligation to tell the truth, especially when you're dealing with living memory. The script I'm currently working on is based on a true story, and I find myself constantly having to check the impulse to rewrite history! Between doing adaptations or rewrites and doing my own stuff, it's weird but there's surprisingly little difference. With the exception of my own second novel, *Paper Mask*, most novels I've adapted are so un-filmic in their structure that you have to deconstruct the book and re-invent the story. *The Far Side of the World* was a case in point.

What did you like to read when you were growing up and how did it impact your writing/storytelling style as an adult?
I read Steinbeck, Jack London, Hemingway, and Graham Greene. I liked strong

narratives with a sense of authentic lived experience. That's what I always try to write.

What's the first thing you ever sold and how long had you been writing prior to the sale?
I trained as a doctor and that was my job off and on until six or seven years ago. I sold a short story when I was 26, then took a few months out to write my first novel, *Kingsley's Touch*, which was finally published three years later. I wrote two more novels after that, but kept going back to medicine.

Why did you decide to become a writer?
I'm a romantic. I was in love with the idea of the solitary dreamer who travels the world, sees everything, understands everything, and writes about it. Of course being a writer is nothing like that....

Complete this sentence: If I weren't a writer, I would be _____.
Still a doctor, I guess. Probably doing aid work in the third world, which is what I was doing up to nine years ago when we had our first child and I had to start making money.
(**Author note: Collee and his wife, Debs, moved to Sydney, Australia in 1996 where they are raising their three children, Lauren, Isla, and Jack.**)

What are you working on now?
Another war movie, this time for Stephen Spielberg. It's a Fox Dreamworks co-production.

If you could adapt any existing novel to a feature film and cast it with whomever you wanted, what would it be and who would star?
I'd write a film about the homecoming of Odysseus and I'd cast Liam Neeson. Actually I wrote this already for Fox Searchlight. Edward Bond rewrote it and Neil Jordan is doing another rewrite. They're still trying to pull together funding. That's the business.

What's the best career advice that anyone ever gave you?

"You have to enjoy the process." Once a film is written, it's out of your hands and the chances are that it will never get made. You have to enjoy the process of researching and writing and discussing and rewriting a story until it's as perfect as you can make it. If you wait for the delayed gratification of seeing your name on screen, you'll wait your whole life and probably die embittered.

And what's the worst advice you ever got?

"It's a great idea — keep it to yourself." We're social animals. I no longer see writing as a solitary profession. Fictional ideas grow and flourish when you talk about them and share them. They die when you get protective and secretive. Film writing is the best fun because it's so collaborative and pitching a story to everyone who will listen is the best way I know to enhance the storyline. Being obsessive and solitary is the best way to kill it.

What words of wisdom would you like to leave with new writers who are still struggling to find their own voices?

Forget your own voice. Write something mainstream and entertaining. Work with people you like.

CHAPTER 4 | CONFLICT MANAGEMENT & THE VIEW FROM HERE

In the time of the ancient Greeks, the gist of their dramatic performances focused on man versus the gods. By Shakespeare's era, stories about man versus other men gave royals and peasantry alike something tangible to relate to. By the turn of the 20th century, storytellers had found yet another mercurial enemy with whom man could wage battle; specifically, himself.

What do these three diverse venues have in common? The answer is conflict, the most critical ingredient in keeping audiences glued to their seats. In order to make that conflict credible, of course, you need to be able to identify which of your characters has the most persuasive voice to deliver it and how much he or she will be transformed by story's end.

WHAT CONSTITUTES CONFLICT?

The crux of all conflict involves moving your characters from Point A to Point B. Thwarting that journey — whether it be on a physical, emotional, or spiritual plane — are the following obstacles:

> The Ticking Clock Syndrome
  The protagonist has 48 hours to locate a bomb, deliver a
  ransom, rescue a hostage, etc. Example: *Run Lola Run*.
> Mistaken Identity/Identity Theft
  The inability to prove one's true identity places a character in
  comically compromising or life-threatening positions.
  Example: *The Net*.
> Diametrical Differences
  He's Catholic; she's Jewish. He's dead; she's alive. He's married; she's available. Can a relationship be saved if concession
  isn't an option? Example: *The Age Of Innocence*.

> Insufficient Resources
  The protagonist is rich in idealism but light on cash, time,
  manpower, etc., to orchestrate a rebellion, a takeover, or
  preservation of the status quo. Example: *Braveheart*.
> Trading Places
  The lead character is empathy-deficient until he/she is forced
  to experience life through the eyes of another.
  Example: *Freaky Friday*.
> Straying Hearts
  You can love some of the people all of the time and all of the
  people some of the time. It just gets messy when they find
  out about each other. Example: *Fatal Attraction*.
> The Isolation Factor/Fish Out of Water
  Whether the label of loneliness is self-imposed or ascribed
  by society, conflict is inevitable when extraordinary people
  attempt to function in an ordinary environment. Example:
  Good Will Hunting. On the flip side, ordinary individuals
  who suddenly are thrust into extraordinary circumstances
  are forced to rise to challenges that life had not previously
  prepared them for. Example: *Star Wars*.

WHAT CONFLICT ISN'T

If "The Big Problem" you have posed could be resolved in just one conversation
between the characters, it's not enough to constitute a full-length script.
Television sitcoms are an example of this, wherein misunderstandings, missteps,
and missed connections all can be fixed in the space of 22 minutes.

Nor is conflict a tableau in which your characters simply sit around Starbucks
wondering whether they should be doing something different with their lives.
In the absence of an inciting incident that will challenge their sensibilities,
pull the rug out from under them, or threaten their existences, they are doing
little more than killing time, time that could be better spent on a story that
has actual substance.

CONFLICT AND THE SOLAR SYSTEM

Unlike real life, which serves up daily a full plate of conflicts for us to juggle, a screenplay centers on one specific problem, a problem around which everything else must revolve. The tendency of fledgling writers to try to mimic the complexities of reality by putting in *more* than one conflict results in a scatter-gun script that misses the mark on all levels.

As of this writing, I am in the midst of revisiting my own fondness for penning "ensemble" works and restructuring a particular story so that the main character's personal crisis is never ignored for more than half a page. Much as I admittedly favor the original version and its more equitable distribution of screen time among the players, it was pointed out to me that, in order for this script to be successfully launched with a name star, the name star needs to be front and center for at least 85% of it. Even a math flunkie can see that this translates to very little time left over for anybody else's dilemmas to be examined, much less resolved.

In order to put this requirement in perspective, think of your central conflict as the sun. Think of Earth as your main character, subjected to moments of light and dark pursuant to his/her invariable rotation. The rest of the planets are the other characters and extraneous issues in your protagonist's life. While he or she is always aware of their presence and their respective proximity to the central issue, a decision to break formation and revolve around Pluto for a while or to go count rings around Saturn simply never comes up. A situation that occurs on Venus is likewise only of significance if it in some way impacts what Venus and Earth both have in common; specifically, their orbits around the sun.

Let's say that your story is about a new employee named Ernie who is madly in love with his boss' daughter. She is, literally, the center of his whole universe. Everything that he does relates to his quest for a happily-ever-after with her.

While Ernie's life is peopled with a lot of colorful characters, you need to resist the temptation to let Ernie wander off and go schlep their emotional baggage for them. Why? Because it detracts from his primary objective of pursuing his damsel fair. What you *can* let Ernie do, though, is allow him to engage in peripheral conflicts that will ultimately advance his own cause.

For example:

> As a new employee, Ernie's abilities and reputation are under scrutiny. He needs to make a good impression with the boss who, hopefully, will perceive him as quality son-in-law material and ultimately give the relationship his blessing.
> He needs to vanquish his rival who works for the same firm. Again, the actions in which he engages to accomplish this serve the twofold purpose of impressing his lady-love and her father, as well as dispatching the competition.
> He also needs to land a major account that will solidify his professional standing with the firm, provide the financial wherewithal to start a comfortable life with the girl he loves, and affirm his own faith that he can accomplish anything he sets his mind to.

Much as you might like to weave in backstory elements of Ernie's prior relationships with other women, his estrangement from his older brother, his roommate's bouts with alcoholism, his cleaning lady's impending deportation to Uruguay, or even the weekends he selflessly spends making recordings for the blind, none of them has any bearing on whether he gets the girl and makes that long-sought trip to the altar.

POINTS TO PONDER
> What is the central conflict of your own movie idea?
> Is it of sufficient sustainability to fill 1-1/2 to 2 hours of screen time? If not, could it work as a short?
> From the earlier list in this chapter, what type of conflict is it?
> How is your idea similar to the sample movie identified for that type of conflict? How is it different?

> Identify three peripheral conflicts that will directly or indi-
> rectly impact the resolution of the main problem being
> addressed in your film.

WHOSE STORY IS IT ANYWAY?

As anyone who has ever grown up with siblings can easily attest, there are always
at least three versions of any given incident: (1) their story, (2) your story, and (3)
what *really* happened. Throw in the observations of other household members,
eavesdropping neighbors, casual passers-by and even the family pet and that single incident can be interpreted in any number of different ways.

A screenplay is subject to the same level of viewpoint variety. It just depends on
whose rendition you — as the author — would like it to be.

In Amadeus, *the story of Mozart's musical genius is told in flashback through the viewpoint of his court rival,
Antonio Salieri, played by F. Murray Abraham. (*Amadeus, *Saul Zaentz Company, 1984.)*

Let's say that you've decided to adapt *Little Red Riding Hood* into a feature film.
In its original fairy tale format, the viewpoint is omnipresent; we see the plot
unfold from the narrator's third-person perspective. Although Red herself is the
title character, she is only knowledgeable of those scenes in which she personally
participates. Accordingly, her presumably innocent disclosure that she is on her

way to her grandmother's house can be construed as either a polite way to get the wolf to buzz off or a carefully orchestrated set-up to dispatch a relative she wasn't particularly fond of anyway.

"Did I mention that she's frail and helpless and lives alone?" Red tells him. "Here, let me write down the address for you... "

How would the telling of the tale be different from the standpoint of the wolf? Certainly as a creature at the top of the forest food chain, he wouldn't be very likely to judge his acts as criminal behavior. After all, a wolf's gotta do what a wolf's gotta do, right? Since his first opportunity to make a meal of Red didn't work out, he resorts to his next available option: a granny snack down the road.

But what if he were trying to *warn* the grandmother that the woodsman who worked in her neighborhood was, in actuality, a serial killer? Motivated by his desperation to save the old woman's life, the only safe hiding place Mr. Wolf could think of on such short notice was... in his stomach. (Doesn't the fact he swallowed her whole suggest it was just a temporary plan?)

What about the character of the grandmother? Was she just a victim of her own naiveté in opening the front door without first establishing who was there? Perhaps if we heard the story from *her* side of things, we'd learn that Red's motivation in bringing fattening treats every week was to hasten her elderly relative's demise so as to inherit that sweet little cottage on a prime piece of real estate. Annoyed with such duplicity, the grandmother hired a contract killer in the form of a local carnivore, little knowing that the latter had his own spin on the phrase "meal ticket."

Last but not least, we have the woodsman who just happened to be wandering by an open window in time to overhear the wolf's remarks about big ears and big eyes. Recognizing that young Red had about as much on the ball as Lois Lane when it came to seeing through lame disguises, he immediately sprang into action.

What was his real motivation, though? Was it to dazzle Red into accepting an on-the-spot marriage proposal? Was he already engaged in a clandestine relationship with the grandmother and startled to discover that their afternoon tryst had been pre-empted by a wolf wearing her nightgown? Or were he and the wolf secret partners in crime, preying on the confidence and ignorance of the fairer sex to advance their own agendas?

We'll never know the answer, of course, since we only heard the story from one side: the one that the author chose for us.

As screenwriters, you, too, will be vested with choosing just one side from many. How you know whether you've selected the *best* one derives from one or more of the following criteria:

> LIKABILITY QUOTIENT

Audiences want someone they can root for, generally someone who is also likable and with whom they'd enjoy having lunch or grabbing a few beers after work. Film, after all, is the vicarious canvas on which audiences project their own hopes, dreams, triumphs. In addition, their affinity for affable underdogs allows them to reflect on the times in their lives that they themselves have felt as if the odds were stacked against them. That's not to say, of course, that you couldn't also craft a story with a perfectly likable *villain* at its helm. As long as he or she embraces ambitions or relates experiences which will resonate with a sympathetic audience, there's no reason a bad guy can't be centerstage.

> DEGREE OF RISK

Who has the most to lose in your story? If a character doesn't put very much on the line, you can't expect an audience to invest very much interest in the outcome. We want to see what's at stake and we want to understand its significance from the standpoint of the person taking the biggest risk to win it, protect it, or just get it back.

> DEGREE OF THREAT

Bond. James Bond. Why do we like to view events through the eyes of this super-sleuth? Because he's all that stands in the way between evil-doers and their schemes for world domination. Not only do we warm to characters who *know* that they are thorns in the enemies' sides, but also to those who unwittingly witness criminal acts and *don't* know just how much trouble will be unleashed as a result of their being in the wrong place at the wrong time.

> QUEST FOR REDEMPTION

Hand in hand with an audience's love for the underdog is its empathy for those who learn to forgive themselves through acts that redeem past errors and omissions. The firefighter who couldn't save the life of his own child, the ballplayer who cost the home team a winning game, the woman whose fear of driving kept her from getting a sick relative to the hospital — these and other characters whose mettle will be tested in new crises are always good choices for the prominent point of view.

FRONT AND CENTER

Based on the above criteria, which character in your movie idea is the best one to "tell" the story? Why is this character the best choice?

CONFLICT AND THE CHARACTER ARC

Whatever the crisis besetting your protagonists, they're not likely to be exactly the same people at the end of the journey that they were when the trip first began. Whether their efforts are rewarded or squelched, the events in which they participate for the movie's duration play a part in shaping and reshaping their views about the world, their peers, and even themselves. Such transition is referred to as the character arc.

The character arc is the degree of emotional growth which he or she undergoes as a result of success or failure. While physical changes can occur, too, as a product of aging or accident, it is a character's psyche in relation to predictability, adaptation, and ambiguity that determines whether the role will become a memorable one in the minds of the audience.

How much — or how little — your characters evolve can be whimsically categorized as:
1. Easter Islanders
2. Play-Dohs
3. Lava Lamps

EASTER ISLANDERS

For centuries, people have been intrigued by the immense statues of stone located on Easter Island in the Pacific. Who carved these big cement-heads? How did they get there? What does it all mean? Neither time nor Mother Nature have rendered much impact on them nor diluted their mystique, making them a presence with unquestionable staying power.

Characters whose value systems and opinions are as chiseled in stone as the monoliths on Easter Island have a staying power, as well. Why? Because no matter what conflicts they are forced to weather, they still will be rooted exactly where we left them when the fight is over. In other words, they are built to *withstand* all external elements.

Although their character arcs barely register as blips on the radar screen, audiences don't mind because the predictability factor inherent in the players' behavior projects a comfort level they can sit back and enjoy. Audiences readily warm to the notion that this hero or heroine won't stray from whatever has been introduced at the outset; what they see is exactly what they are going to get. Indiana

Jones, for instance, isn't likely to deviate left or right of his centered philosophy that ancient artifacts belong in a museum and that women belong in the background.

Not surprisingly, Easter Islander personas are the most likely candidates to end up in film sequels or television spin-offs, Fraiser Crane being an example of the latter.

PLAY-DOHS

At the opposite end of the spectrum are the Play-Dohs. Play-Doh®, for the uninitiated, is a soft clay substance that — unlike real clay — doesn't harden, affording youngsters hours of creative invention. By the end of the play period, the innocuous little lump that started out as one thing will have been dropped, stretched, squeezed, rolled, squished, tossed, pounded, divided, multiplied, and reshaped into something else.

The correlation to the characters in your script is that their personalities are still malleable enough to react to a gamut of external forces and, thus, undergo the necessary changes to adapt to new circumstances and responsibilities.

Jamie Lee Curtis in *True Lies* is a quintessential Play-Doh. When we first meet her character, Helen, we see that she is a wife, a mother, and a legal secretary who yearns for a little excitement in an existence that she thinks has become pretty darned dull. She gets her wish, not only with the discovery that her husband is actually a spy but that his enemies mistakenly assume she is secret agent, as well. Helen's dormant energies and resourcefulness, coupled with a renewed passion for her spouse, change her from dowdy to dazzling.

The majority of films embrace this Play-Doh mode of emotional evolution; i.e., the miser who turns generous (*A Christmas Carol*), the pal who learns to let go (*My Best Friend's Wedding*), the workaholic who finally finds romance with the girl next door (*Sabrina*).

The reinvented Helen (Jamie Lee Curtis) shows husband Harry (Arnold Schwarzenegger) that he's met his match in undercover partners. (True Lies, 20th Century Fox, 1994)

In each case, the decision to change one's behavior or outlook is predicated upon what he/she stands to lose by staying the same, thus creating the requisite suspense and speculation on the part of the viewers.

LAVA LAMPS

Harder to gauge in terms of personal growth are the Lava Lamps. A product of the psychedelic 1960s, real lava lamps are a mesmerizing study-in-motion, the globules perpetually separating, free-floating, and reconnecting as a result of heat. We really don't know what they're going to do next and, frankly, neither do they. The fact that these globules (emotions) are in a self-contained environment also means that they act *independently* of the external setting in which the lamp itself resides.

Further, the amount of attention all of this internal churning will get from others is contingent upon the backdrop. If the setting is the 1960s for instance, the movement will go virtually unnoticed because it fits in with everything else.

Centerstage in a Victorian parlor or a conference room in the 1990s, however, it will garner odd looks and confusion until its presence is explained or removed.

Kevin Costner's performance in *Dances with Wolves* is a good lava lamp example. No matter what setting he is placed in, the need to reconcile his inner demons is fated to be a work-in-progress. Just when things seem to have acquiesced and oozed into a cohesive mass, another facet of his psyche emerges and breaks loose. Therefore, whatever "progress" is made is countered by ongoing displays of back-tracking, ambiguity, and self-doubt.

With Easter Islanders and Play-Dohs, we can generally predict what the characters' lives might be like after the movie is over. With lava lamps, it's anyone's guess. That's what makes them such compelling enigmas.

ANALYZING CHARACTER ARCS
WITHIN YOUR OWN SCREENPLAY

> Describe what your protagonist is like as a person when we first meet him or her. What does he or she want the very most when the story begins?
> Will your character stay true to this objective all the way through the story? Why or why not?
> Which of the three character arcs best fits your protagonist's emotional journey through the story?
> Will he or she achieve the desired outcome? Will it be less? Will it be more?
> Does your protagonist's character arc lend itself to a sequel? Why or why not?

AGENTS FOR CHANGE

At the start of the story, the protagonist's point of view stems from where he or she is at that particular moment in time. Maybe they are content with the status quo and abhor the idea of any revision to it. On the other hand, maybe they're desperate to be somewhere else or to acquire something they're presently lacking. What will it take to light a fire under them and force a decision about their future?

In order to chart a new course and alter his or her current perspective, what your lead character needs is to be introduced to a catalyst, an agent for change.

The agent for change is an individual whose own point of view (or personal circumstance) is often in contrast to the protagonist. While agents for change have well-defined goals and objectives of their own, they generally don't have to undergo any character transformations themselves in order to achieve those quests. Instead the agent for change is responsible, either by design or accident, for setting up the requisite strategies and events which will impact the hero/heroine's growth — or lack of it — during the course of the central conflict.

The classic *Casablanca* is a nice demonstration of how this works. Although there is a strong undercurrent of romance between Rick and Ilsa, the story is related to us through Rick's viewpoint. Here is a man who has basically declared himself neutral while the world around him is gripped in the grim reality of war.

Enter Ilsa, the agent for change. Ilsa is as determined to be proactive in securing the necessary letters of transit to save her husband, Laszlo, as Rick is steadfast to stay passive, cynical, and not stick his head out for anybody. By the final credits, Ilsa has not only achieved her objective of getting safe passage but also influenced Rick to rejoin humanity and take up a cause that is higher than his own self-interests or the feelings they have for each other.

QUICK QUIZ

Identify the agents for change in each of the following films:
> *Witness*
> *Shakespeare In Love*
> *Moonstruck*
> *Shrek*
> *Rainman*
> *My Best Friend's Wedding*

CONFLICT RESOLUTION

It was impressed upon me by my third grade teacher, Miss Frederickson, that a person should never start something unless he or she intends to finish it. She especially drilled this point home when it came to writing short stories, emphasizing that the worst way you could cheat a reader was to have your characters engage in life-endangering adventures and thrills... only to wake up and reveal that the entire thing had all been a dream.

To this day, I still cringe whenever I read screenplays that build up to a pulse-pounding do-or-die confrontation, only to dribble off into an ending that's just not worthy. While that's not to say that every finale has to be upbeat and Disneyesque in order to be satisfying, it nevertheless needs to answer whatever question lured us in at the outset.

Essentially, conflict resolution follows one of two patterns, depending on whether the protagonist's objective is to vanquish a real or perceived enemy or to conquer a reluctant heart.

In the case of triumphing over an enemy, the formula to remember is:

FLIGHT > FRIGHT > FIGHT

Initially, the hero's reaction to a problem that's not of his own making is to get away from it as fast as possible. Once it becomes apparent that the problem is unavoidable, he then is forced to face up to the fears that made him want to run away. Resolute to conquer his fears in the interests of a higher good, he is finally able to charge into the fray. Whether he lives or dies as a result of this action is of less importance than the fact he took a definitive stand.

For stories of romance, the pattern can be remembered as:

REND > BLEND > MEND

When first we meet the two main characters, they are figuratively at each other's throats. Their pronounced differences make them the least likely pair to ever find common ground. Yet find it they do. He learns that she was neglected as a child, a condition that he can relate to as a youngster who had workaholic parents. She discovers that he throws coins in wishing wells when he thinks no one is looking, an endearing trait that coincides with her secret prayers for a knight in shining armor. When they finally get together, it is a result of acknowledging each other's differences as a strength, not as a bone of contention.

Even if you are planning to leave your movie as an open-ended proposition, paving the way for a sequel, it still needs to be resolved within the framework you have laid out. There needs to be some sort of emotional payoff for audiences that will make them want to come back for more, not scratching their heads and wondering why they sat through this one.

HOW DOES IT END?
> Are your lead characters proactive in bringing about the story's resolution?
> How will your story end?
> Does it satisfy the question(s) presented by the central conflict?
> Identify two alternative endings for the same story.

CHAPTER 5 | THE AUDIENCE MINDSET: WHAT'S IN IT FOR ME?

In even the worst years of economic depression, there are two types of businesses that always thrive: bars and theaters. One of them serves spirits, the other uplifts spirits, providing tickets to escape from the woes of a troubled world, if only on a temporary basis.

Like everything else, going to the movies has gotten more expensive. In large part, of course, it's because the business of *making* movies has gotten more expensive. When we read all the hype surrounding an upcoming blockbuster with a nine-figure production price tag, we automatically embrace the expectation that it will give us our money's worth as its audience.

Will we come away from the experience with the satisfaction of having been entertained, educated, enlightened, terrified, or inspired by what that film delivered? Or will we shake our heads in annoyance as we leave the lobby, opining that not only did we just waste $10 but that the studio which produced it blew a whopping $100 million?

Why do some movies work and others don't? The bottom line is that their success or failure rests entirely with the audience. Even the most jaded critics will still forgive a multitude of technological sins if the core story is one that has the capacity to stir emotions. Whether a film is able to accomplish this objective depends on the amount of relevance that viewers can attach to their own lives, dreams, and insecurities.

> Love stories work because we can all identify with the quest to find ever-lasting romance and companionship... and the pain of letting it go.

> Action stories work because they allow us to vicariously step into the shoes of someone whose life is more exciting and risk oriented than our own.
> Horror stories work because of their power to conjure up our childhood fears of hungry monsters lurking under the bed.

What about those plots, however, that unfold in a time or setting with which we have a limited frame of reference or emotional connection?

Colorado in the 1870s, for example. On the surface, is this an era and locale we'd eagerly flock to for entertainment?

One of the most popular lectures I give in my workshops relates to the 1990s television series, *Dr. Quinn, Medicine Woman*. For those of you unfamiliar with the premise, it starred Jane Seymour as a woman doctor who travels west to Colorado to set up a medical practice. Not only does she encounter distrust and discrimination because of her sex but assumes the unbidden role of motherhood when one of her dying patients leaves her custody of three children. Compounding Micaela Quinn's problems is her attraction to a brooding loner in buckskin who would raise eyebrows among her blueblood family back East and most assuredly be flummoxed by the correct fork to use at dinner.

Could this same set-up have worked in 1890s Chicago, 1960s South America, or the Planet Pluto in the 26th century? Absolutely. The physical place and time become immaterial as long as the characters are waging battle with the very same issues that confront and confound contemporary audiences: racism, sexism, oppression, passion, death, self-doubt, parenthood, jealousy, isolation, substance abuse, violence, coming of age, guilt, etc.

Did any of us care about ancient Rome until Russell Crowe donned a toga in *Gladiator*? For that matter, did we become obsessed with ancient Rome and start buying mail-order statuary from the Toscano® catalogue *after* the final credits? Of course not. What lingered, however, was our empathy for the valiant warrior whom Crowe depicted, a man driven to avenge the wrongs he was dealt by his enemy. Whether a hero's noble acts are carried out in the Coliseum of Rome, in the Highlands of Scotland, or on the shores of Normandy, it is his perseverance and triumph that we universally cheer for and remember, not the backdrop it was played against.

To illustrate the importance of appealing to audiences on a personal level they can relate to, I had the privilege of interviewing eight screenwriters whose historically based works have garnered award and recognition in such prestigious competitions as the Chesterfield, Nicholl Fellowships, Project Greenlight, CAPE Foundation and *Scr(i)pt Magazine's* Open Door, to name a few.

Each participant was asked the same three questions:
> What inspired you to write this particular story?
> What was the biggest challenge in structuring it for the screen?
> What aspect of it will resonate with today's movie-goers?

Their responses reflect a correlation between what the inspired event or persona of the past said to them as authors and how that message was played back in the context of a visual medium targeted to a modern-thinking public.

As you read their replies, keep in mind that these are all men and women just like you who sat down one day, decided to write scripts based on events that captured their attention, and submitted the finished products to competitions. Will your name be added to the next list of award-winning screenwriters? As they say, you can't win a contest if you don't enter it!

Film Title: *Deborah Samson*
Screenwriter: John Walker Bellingham
Circa: American Revolutionary War
Premise: The true story of the first American woman combat soldier who enlisted disguised as a man during the Revolutionary War, served three years before being discovered, was wounded twice. She was also the first woman to earn a

livelihood as a public speaker and is the official heroine of the state of Massachusetts.

> *A friend gave me a book called, "Letters To A Nation," and I read a letter in there written by Paul Revere around 1810, who was writing to Congress on behalf of his neighbor, Deborah Samson Gannett. She was in need of a military pension as she had served heroically in the military during the Revolution disguised as a man. I found it such a fascinating story that I researched it as much as I could and then wrote the script, adding in some romance, of course.*

> *The biggest challenge I found in writing this script was keeping the story as true to history as possible, yet, making it commercially palatable. One Hollywood script consultant was adamant that I change the ending to fit a more formulaic Hollywood conclusion. Yet, women who read the script seemed to feel quite the opposite. I stayed with my gut; yet, I suppose it could change, since it is currently making the large studio rounds.*

> *Audience appeal? Historical context in the modern paradigm. The producer who currently is working on the script feels the material is timeless and not limited to its chronology. I agree with her. She feels that the message that girls/women can do as well as men or better in any endeavor has no boundaries. And what was possible then is even more possible now.*

Film Title: *Gunfighters' Surgeon*
Screenwriter: Douglas Raine
Circa: 1870-1910
Premise: True story of America's first trauma surgeon, who pioneered antiseptic, reconstructive, and teaching surgeries while battling established medical beliefs and his own alcoholism.

My great granduncle (William MacLeod Raine) wrote over 80 western stories in the early 1900s, so, I've always loved westerns.

I was asked to proofread an article about Dr. George Goodfellow, America's first trauma surgeon, and found the material fascinating. The more research I did, the more I realized that Goodfellow was truly an unsung hero of the West.

A lot of the material written about Dr. Goodfellow was hearsay and legend. I wanted to stay as true to the story as possible but there were major areas of his life with no documentation (in particular his wife's illness). All of his journals were destroyed in the San Francisco earthquake. There are only a half dozen published papers, his diary from when he was 12 years old and some legal documents. I did a geographic and sociological timeline of his life. With the aid of other diaries from that time period and interviewing specialists in medical history, I was able to fill in most of the gaps. Fortunately, Goodfellow's life had crossed paths with many other notable figures, so that became an additional referencing point. The first draft was very "episodic" as one reader said. I manipulated a couple facts to create a "through line" for the screenplay and a stronger story. The story, visuals, and dialogue have received the most praise. The dialogue I fashioned from a mixture of Goodfellow's writings and dialogue (mostly the cadence and verbiage) from my great uncle's early westerns. Knowing the background of the characters helped to give each his own voice.

What struck me most were the parallels that could be drawn to our lifestyle today. Goodfellow battled against his own alcoholism, STDs, and racism. There was rampant gun violence and segregation. Towns erupted so quickly there was very little infrastructure to support them. Views different from those of the "establishment" were stifled. Yet, perseverance can still triumph and the smallest amount of good that you do will get noticed. Goodfellow believed that a doctor should learn something from every patient... if not from the operation itself, then something about the patients, how they live, their beliefs. The message to the audience? Learn all that you can from all that is around you.

Film Title: *Impression*
Screenwriter: Kate Maney
Circa: 1874
Premise: *Impression* is based on the true story of artist Berthe Morisot, her ill-fated love affair with the renowned painter Eduoard Manet, and her emergence as one of the leaders of the French Impressionist movement.

In the mid-80s there was a touring exhibit of Impressionist paintings which included works from all nine exhibits in chronological order. In going through the exhibit, and reading the descriptions of the artists by their paintings, I was struck by one that said, "There is a woman in the group, as there is in all celebrated gangs. Her name is Berthe Morisot, and she is interesting to watch. Her feminine grace lives amid the excesses of a frenzied mind." This stuck with me and, while studying screenwriting at UCLA, I decided to research Morisot and develop a screenplay about her life. So, while it specifically wasn't a time period, but rather a historical personality, that motivated my decision, because Morisot's story is also the story of birth of the Impressionist movement, a lot of the script visuals echo the same visuals the artists of the time were painting, such as the Gare St. Lazare enveloped in smoke by Monet and Renoir's paintings of outdoor dancing.

Historical accuracy versus dramatic structure/tension was my biggest challenge. This is a biggie. First of all, since nobody really knows all the details, a lot of dramatic license has to be used in simply crafting dialogue and depicting actions. For example, there is no proof that Berthe Morisot had a love affair with Eduoard Manet. This has just been inferred from his intimate portraits of her and the fact her journals covering the time period when they were likely the closest are lost or have been destroyed. Were they really lovers? Who knows? Does it make a better story if they were — absolutely! In terms of dramatic structure, it works better to have the story take place in a shorter time period than the actual events took — and frequently, it flows better to rearrange the events for a more dramatic arc. Similarly, it is often necessary to cut and/or combine some of the people involved to make the film easier to follow. Again, you have to give up historical accuracy in these instances to make a better film. The main concern for the filmmaker, I think, is to simply stay as close to the essence of the historical figure/historical time, while also making the best film possible in terms of dramatic structure and the emotional ride you take your audience on.

Impression is set in an occupied wartime France, after the overthrow of the last Napoleon. It is still a time when women had a very restricted role in society. So, while audiences in the U.S. or Western Europe may not see a lot of similarities, Middle Eastern or some Far Eastern audiences may see more of a reflection of their present-day societies, both political and social. That said, no matter the historical context, some things always will continue to resonate in terms of the human condition: The bittersweet emotions of falling in love with the wrong man; The difficult decision of choosing career versus marriage; striving to achieve a personal goal seemingly out of reach; continuing to try against reason, against societal acceptance, and not listening to those naysayers who try to keep you down. In these ways, Impression *is a modern story, a very human story and an inspirational story, no matter what the time period.*

Film Title: *Last Chance, Wyoming*
Screenwriter: Kristin Kirby
Circa: 1885
Premise: A gutsy female journalist in 1885 New York heads out West and runs smack into outlaws and unscrupulous fossil hunters, falls in love with two rivals, and starts running the local newspaper.

I was fascinated by the juxtaposition of the true events I was writing about, that in the middle of the Wild West in the 1870s and 1880s — with such primitive conditions, outlaws robbing banks and trains, whites and Native Americans still at war — scientists were out in the middle of all this searching for dinosaur fossils and discovering new species. We usually equate that activity with the modern world and yet this was really happening in the West at the time.

The biggest challenge was picking and choosing from all my research! I wanted to include everything — the colloquialisms of the time, the everyday things people did, as well as the broader historical events. My first few drafts were chock full of historical stuff, which made them a bit clumsy to handle. I had to pick only what served my story and didn't bog it down. Another part of that challenge was condensing the events, in this case, the real life feud of scientists Edward Drinker Cope and Othniel Charles Marsh as they scoured the American West in search of dinosaur fossils. This resulted in a shorter, more dramatic, time frame, condensing it from around 30 years to less than a year. I also chose to fictionalize the historical figures I researched; I felt this gave me more freedom to change things around and make a more cohesive story.

As for audience identification, the obvious answer is that science was a part of people's lives in 1885 just like it is today. With exciting discoveries happening all the time and technology and inventions coming so fast, people often worried where it all would lead. Combine this with a rising population of different races all jostled together and trying to get along. Things haven't changed as much in the modern world as we think they have. We're still encountering the same issues.

Film Title: *Bitter Lake*
Screenwriter: Devin Wallace
Circa: 1893
Premise: When a black detective from New York disappears while working undercover in Alabama (pursuing a black Robin Hood folk hero), his wife sets off on a dangerous quest to learn what happened.

I had known this marvelous old folk song, "Railroad Bill," about a turn-of-the-century African American outlaw, a Robin Hood-like figure, since I was a kid. In 1992 I got a grant from the National Endowment for the Arts to write and direct a new radio play, so I started digging around for historical information about this character. The search led me back to Alabama and Florida in the 1890s. It was a fascinating period of time, particularly in terms of black-white relations in the South. Railroad Bill became a powerful symbol for African Americans, as he eluded some of the biggest manhunts ever conducted and shared his train-robbing spoils with impoverished black sharecroppers. The other thing I stumbled onto in my research that interested me was the fact that a black detective from the North was hired to infiltrate Railroad Bill's gang. He was successful, and was working on setting up a trap with the authorities when he disappeared. There weren't many African Americans employed as professional detectives in those days and I wondered what it would have been like for him to go south, and find that the man he was tracking was not just some criminal, but a powerful symbol of black resistance, as well.

I think the biggest challenge in any historical drama is trying to catch the atmosphere and psychology of the time period and the place. The historical immersion process however, is my favorite part of writing.

Most people don't know about the convict lease law of the period, which enabled the state to farm out prisoners to labor camps. It was, basically, a crafty substitute for slavery, as many black men were arrested, often on minor or trumped up charges, and literally worked to death at camps that were unregulated by the states. Twenty-five years after the Civil War, life was a very tough proposition for African Americans in the South. This time period is rarely covered in film, and I believe people find it interesting in that it adds to their understanding of our nation's history.

Film Title: *The Red Snow*
Screenwriter: Shinho Lee
Circa: 1911-1945
Premise: When a Korean-American mother reveals her life as a comfort woman to her son, he learns the tragic story of her love affair with a Japanese officer, the life-long friend she lost, and the survivor's guilt she has battled ever since.

> *As a Korean artist, I felt a sense of duty to re-explore the experience of the Japanese occupation of my country. This was mainly because this period (1911-1945) has been largely forgotten or consciously swept aside by modern Koreans anxious to move forward. Internationally it has, perhaps, always been overshadowed by the Korean War, which followed shortly thereafter. Yet, the legacies of that occupation still can be seen in Korean society today and I wanted to find a way to examine these difficult times.*

> *My biggest challenge? Having met with former Korean comfort women and having researched their real stories, I wanted to ensure that my screenplay was both a truthful and accurate testament to those who survived, but also that it was very clearly my own personal reflection on these events. Writing in English, I had to work hard to recreate the attitudes, behavior, and sensibility of the period and specific characters. I also had to discover how to dramatize the voices and experiences of my characters accurately but in ways which would be accessible to, and resonate with, modern international audiences.*

> *My screenplay is written from the perspective of two women. While their stories are told at a specific period in Korean history, the persecution, abuse, and total disempowerment these two characters suffer at this time are also experiences which many women have endured throughout history, regardless of culture*

or geography. For me, the struggles of my characters represent the similar plight of many women in the world today.

Film Title: *Semper Fi*
By D. Jay Williams
Circa: 1969
Premise: Two young men test their values and lifetime friendship through the crucible of war and change — for better and worse.

Semper Fi *is based on my tour in Viet Nam as a member of Echo Company, Second Battalion, Fourth Marines. I wasn't an especially effective Marine (which the script bares out and explores), but I did serve with a storied group of guys. Books have been written about this small group of 150 men including one especially well received, "The Proud Bastards" by Mr. Michael Helms. He was also a rifleman of this company. In 1999 I joined a VA council group for troubled Viet Nam vets and* Semper Fi *originated as a writing assignment as part of that program. It started out as a four-line poem, but somehow over the course of a year it grew into a 117-page script!*

It is difficult to take a true story that encompasses several months and tell it concisely and dramatically within the confines of a two-hour Hollywood movie. If you have more than eight or 10 prominently recurring characters, you will confuse and lose your audience. So I had to pare down the number of people important to my story by, in some cases, combining two and three of them into one person. I had no choice. And I had no choice but to reorder some of the events; what happened over the course of time and several combat patrols is sometimes condensed into one day. If I had been writing a book or a documentary (or if Hollywood were to allow us 300 pages!), I wouldn't have had to do that either. Another problem is that real life doesn't have the tidy character arcs and resolutions required for the screen. There were cases where I took some literary license and colored in motivations or exaggerated conflicts. And the character representing me (I changed nearly everyone's name) was given a denouement that I didn't especially earn. In the end I was faithful enough to the story that fellow members of Echo Company would recognize that it was a story about them. I was as historically accurate as this art form permits.

Story telling is required by human beings; it's part of our gene makeup. We use stories to sort out our values and to encourage ourselves to prevail in trial and hardship. And even to assuage ourselves to our own ultimate demise. So it's not surprising that many of the best stories are about war. We can all agree that war is bad, but it gives us some of our greatest examples of honor, courage, and sacrifice — and even redemption. I've never met people who better exemplified these attributes than this group of Marines, and so in honor of them I wrote Semper Fi.

Film Title: *Tiananmen*
Screenwriter: Bill Flannigan
Circa: 1989
Premise: A cynical photojournalist working in Asia reluctantly agrees to help an old girlfriend search for her missing Chinese lover, reportedly killed during the brutal government crackdown on demonstrators at Tiananmen Square. Along the way, the two former lovers must come to terms with their conflicting feelings for each other, and the truth about themselves and the people they've chosen to love.

My initial inspiration for this screenplay was a documentary that I saw. Also, I was a Chinese Studies major in school, and was living in Asia during the events leading up to the Tiananmen massacre. Since I speak Chinese and have many Chinese friends, the topic was very close to me and really needed to be told.

Finding a way to bring Westerners into the story in an organic way was the biggest obstacle. I knew that trying to tell the story with just Chinese characters would be a difficult sell, so I had to have at least one — and it turns out two — of my lead roles be either American or European. Using them as vehicles helped to tell the story to readers who might not be as familiar with the events surrounding Tiananmen. Also, I didn't want to preach politics and history, so I needed to come up with a love story — a love triangle actually — that would carry the narrative, while not getting bogged down in the details of the story.

The 15-year anniversary of this event will be Spring of 2004. I think the thing that will resonate with modern audiences is the realization that liberty and freedom are still rare things in the world today, and that people quietly do heroic things every day, unnoticed and away from the spotlight. I wanted to show through my protagonist, Henri, that a single person can make a difference but only by getting personally committed and involved. The first line of the script spells this out when a character tells Henri that someday he'll have to put down his camera and get dirty. I think audiences will respond to this notion that change only occurs when we stop observing and start getting involved.

The world's most famous playwright has made a fair number of appearances throughout modern cinema. As you've seen from the samples provided in this chapter, the inclusion of historical personages is a challenge that requires the integration of period language and contemporary relevance. (Shakespeare In Love, Bedford Falls Productions/Miramax/Universal, 1998.)

IDEA-STARTERS

> Identify what you consider to be the 10 most significant events or people in history.

> Why do you consider each of these to be important?

> What specific issues regarding these past events or famous people would resonate with contemporary movie-goers?

> How many of these events or biographies have been made into commercially successful films?

> How closely did the screenwriter follow the historical facts in presenting the story in this medium? If liberties were taken, was it to accommodate the resources of the production or the sensibilities/values of the audience who would be seeing it?

> What elements do you think made each of these films a success (i.e., was it the theme, the cast, the special effects)?

> Did the era in which these films were made have any bearing on their popularity upon release?

> If these films were remade today, how would the increased sensitivity to political correctness impact the script content?
> For those films which were not successful, what accounted for the failure of them to attract and sustain a box-office following?
> Has any of the events or biographies on your list *not* been made into a film?
> Based on what you have learned from this chapter, identify the reasons why such films have not been made.
> If it were your assignment to develop one of these events or personages into a feature length motion picture, how would you decide which elements of the event or lifetime were the most important for inclusion?

SECTION 2
WRITING IT DOWN

CHAPTER 6 | TIMING IS EVERYTHING

The good news is that the editor loved the plot. The bad news is that the story was set in Hawaii.

"What's wrong with Hawaii?" you may ask.

The editor was quick to explain that they had just bought another romance novel only two weeks prior that was set on Oahu and would it be possible to please change mine to somewhere else.

Iowa, for instance.

Ordinarily, I would have said yes. I am, after all, the same person who whimsically did a name/city/limb search-and-replace to copy a steamy chapter from one of my novels into another and to this day no one has even noticed. What was problematic in the Hawaii book, however, was the final confrontation scene. Lovely as Iowa may be in landscape, I was pretty certain it didn't have anything comparable to the craggy cliffs of the Pali from which Kamehameha chased his adversaries to their deaths.

I decided to hold out for a different publisher. The second one, however, felt that my heroine was too smart and could I please dumb her up a bit to make her more vulnerable.

I didn't think so.

The third one liked her just the way she was. They also really liked Hawaii. What made them nervous, though, was the fact that in the first scene I killed off the heroine's magician husband in a tank of water. "*Moonlighting* did an episode last week with a magician in a tank of water," they said. "If you could just kill him off in some other way… "

Such is The Author's Curse: no matter how good the story is, sometimes the sale of it is all a matter of timing.

YESTERDAY'S NEWS

Just like fashion, movie trends are transitory. Whatever is in the theaters this month — whether it's aliens, talking babies, or historical epics about sailors or samurais — is going to be passé by the time you script a line, much less get out and pitch it to a producer.

Even if your screenplay is already written and on a bargaining table somewhere, all eyes will be on the box office if a similarly themed film beats you to the punch. This irony even extends to adaptations wherein the source material actually pre-dates your competitor's release.

What can you do about it?

Sadly, nothing much.

While certain genres can accommodate structural and thematic tweaking, those that require the protagonist to work in a specific occupation, live in a specific era, and carry out a specific mission are not as easily reshaped. These are the scripts that get shelved in temporary deference to those whose market value holds more immediate promise for you. The operative word here is "temporary." In keeping with the earlier analogy about fashion, if you hold on to anything long enough, it's only a matter of time that it will come back and look interesting all over again.

As if your fellow writers weren't enough to cause you angst about timing issues, of course, you've also got public opinion, the media, and world events at large to contend with. When *Independence Day* opened, for instance, I recall my nephew's enthusiastic praise of what a "cool" special effect it was to see the White House blown to smithereens.

In the aftermath of September 11th, however, scripts and images depicting hellacious acts of violence, destruction, and terrorism took on a sobering new meaning to filmmakers. Several movies, in fact, were put on hold or significantly edited so as not to upset, offend, or further traumatize a populace who had witnessed the horrors of the real thing.

POPCORN POLITICS

Gauging the mood of the public is never an easy thing, especially when it comes to trying to predict what kind of movies they are likely to flock to. Every four years, though, our national pulse is taken at the polls when we elect a president. As the media becomes more of an influence in our lives, the political process becomes more and more one of carefully crafted messaging, focus groups, and opinion surveys. Long gone are the days of the stump speech and of the impassioned speeches at county fairs that lasted well into the evening. Oratory has given way to sound bites, and these sound bites and well-crafted images can give you a keen insight into the mood of your potential audience, as well.

The Cold War that lasted through much of the post-World War II era is an example of how politics insinuates itself into the psyche of the movie-going public. The decade of the fifties began with the dark *The Third Man*, a tale of intrigue set in post-war Vienna already embracing themes of paranoia and images of a dark, secretive world behind the Iron Curtain that would be retold countless times over the next two decades. Is it any wonder that this would be the decade that would see some of Alfred Hitchcock's most memorable movies such as *Rear Window* and *North By Northwest*?

McCarthyism took its toll on the industry and upon writers during that decade, but with the election of John Fitzgerald Kennedy in 1960, a new sense of optimism swept the country, even if the Cold War would grow to its most menacing stage during the Cuban Missile Crisis of 1962. The paranoia of the fifties gave way to a more robust war against communism in the sixties, just as the old leaders of WWII gave way to a younger group of veterans as embodied by JFK. Dashing secret agents on both the screen and on television visited exotic locales throughout the world, complete with equally exotic toys and very exotic women.

Is it coincidence that one of the classic Cold War movies, *The Manchurian Candidate* aired the same year (1962) as a young Scotsman, Sean Connery, first portrayed Ian Fleming's unforgettable James Bond in *Dr. No*? Forty years later, the almost comic book setting of the most famous secret agent still reminds us all that a martini must be shaken, not stirred.

With the assassination of President Kennedy and the growing quagmire in Vietnam, the mood of the country became restless. The foundations of the past were cracking and the country as a whole began to shake lose its ties to the past. The civil rights movement, the anti-war movement, and a whole lot of other movements involving sex, drugs, and rock and roll now fed the public's psyche.

As we moved to the seventies, movies became more expressive of this new sense in the country. *The Green Berets,* made in 1968, is the only film of note to ever suggest that the Vietnam War was a noble cause. By 1970, *M*A*S*H* was more reflective of the nation's view of war (even though that movie was set in Korea) and through the next several decades treatment of Vietnam remains more cathartic than historic.

The anti-establishment sentiment of the late 1960s and early 1970s manifested itself in far more different ways than the treatment of war. This period can be summed up well when considering that, in 1967, John Wayne and Robert Mitchum stared in *El Dorado*, Robert Redford and Paul Newman starred in *Butch Cassidy and the Sundance Kid* in 1969, and one year later, Wayne again starred in *Rio Lobo*, a film that coincidentally had Robert Mitchum's son Christopher in the cast as a young Confederate soldier returning home from war to face problems in Texas.

Richard Nixon was president during most of this period, from 1968 until his resignation in 1974. Films became increasingly restless, as did the electorate, during this period of time. *Easy Rider* (1969), *Midnight Cowboy* (1969), and *A Clockwork Orange* (1971) pushed the envelope on a variety of themes. Traditional genres of war and police movies, when seen through the eyes of these

Pals to the end. Robert Redford and Paul Newman's portrayal of affable robbers Sundance and Butch not only started the popular trend of "buddy films" but exemplified the anti-establishment era of the late 60s and early 70s. (Butch Cassidy and the Sundance Kid, 20th Century Fox, 1969.)

Americans manifested themselves in such classics as *Patton* (1970) and *Dirty Harry* (1971). While Nixon was to enjoy a landslide victory in 1972, his days were numbered.

By the time Jimmy Carter became president in 1976, the country was ready for a respite from the challenges of the past decade. The first of the cathartic movies about Vietnam, *The Deer Hunter* (1978), *Coming Home* (1978), and *Apocalypse Now* (1979) were produced. For sheer escapism, *Star Wars* was the perfect elixir for an aging population of rebels with a new cause – making money. While Carter may have been the right person to write the final chapter on the Vietnam experience and the Watergate scandal, the American people did not feel he was the right man to stand up to a group of Islamic fundamentalists in Iran. They left that job to Ronald Reagan.

When looking at the relationship between movies, moods, and politics, be careful to recognize that it is not the issues of the day that drive the creative force, it is the sentiment of the public as manifested by the response to these issues that you are trying to tap into. Great events in world history occurred during the eight years Ronald Reagan was president, but it was his effect on the American psyche that produced films such as *Terms of Endearment* (1983), *Moonstruck* (1987), and *Rainman* (1988).

This general sense of satisfaction, certainly peppered by cautionary tails such as *Wall Street* (1987), was transformed into a general malaise by 1992 and once again, not unlike 32 years prior, the public wanted new blood in Washington. William Jefferson Clinton was the person the people chose for that role.

Would movies such as *Dave* (1993) and *The American President* (1995) have been made had George H. W. Bush won the 1992 presidential election? No one knows, but both these films tapped into a sense of detachment from leaders, and disgust with politics as usual, that remains with us to this day.

When Californians decided to elect another actor to run their state in 2003, it was not because of policy or vision, it was because the mood of the people compelled change. While writers today enjoy far more freedoms than did their counterparts 40 years ago, unless you have the resources to film and distribute your movie yourself, that freedom does not extend to making a film that the public is not ready or is unwilling to see.

Put your finger on the pulse. Read letters to the editor in local newspapers, strike up a conversation with the grocery store clerk about something more than how you want your food bagged. Gauge the response of your friends and co-workers to stories that are uplifting, tragic, or uncomfortable. Watch the messaging in political campaigns closely, as Democrats and Republicans alike spend millions of dollars testing themes and ideas before they ever hit the airwaves.

RECOMMENDED READING

If you're interested in studying additional correlations between what's unfolding in real life and how that translates to what develops in "reel" life, take a look at Patrick Robertson's *"Film Facts"* (Publisher: Billboard Books, 2001). It's not only an entertaining compendium of anything and everything you have ever wanted to know about the movie industry, but includes a thematic timeline of how comedies, dramas, Westerns, and every other genre have been represented in terms of percentage between the years 1914 and the 1990s. If you're a whiz with statistical analysis and forecasting, you just might be able to predict what the next top genre will be!

CHAPTER 7 | STORYTELLING STRUCTURE

From as far back as grade school, it has been drilled into us that every story has to have a beginning, a middle, and an end. This three-act structure carries over into the majority of screenwriting texts on today's market where it is re-labeled as Conflict, Complication, and Resolution.

Where many of these texts fall short, however, is in delineating just how much material should comprise each section in order to escalate the suspense and keep the pace briskly moving from start to finish. This chapter invites you to rethink conventional frameworks and learn how to relate your story's events in the most compelling sequence.

LINEAR VS. NON-LINEAR PROGRESSION

When I think back on the various snippets of wisdom I've been given about the writing profession, the best probably came from a high school teacher who simply said, "Always start your story in the right place."

Whether you're writing your first screenplay or your twentieth, of course, that's not always the easiest advice to follow. What *is*, exactly, "the right place?" And how do you know that a different place wouldn't work better?

One thing for certain is that the longer you stare at a blank page or computer screen, desperately trying to summon the words to leap out of your brain and nicely splat themselves into sentences, the greater likelihood that you're trying too hard to force an unworkable chronology. Your subconscious already knows this and yet you stubbornly forge ahead and fight with it, convinced that there's absolutely no other logical point for the action to begin and the dynamics to get underway.

If you're like most writers starting a new project, you've already mapped out most of the storyline in your head. Where that storyline is going to commence, however, is ironically compounded by the fact that you — its creator — not only possess all the personal history on the characters you're going to use but also know how and where they'll ultimately end up as a result of their opinions and decisions.

To illustrate the conundrum that results, I like to use the example of arranged marriages, wherein both parties are told everything there is to know about each other and, like it or not, that this relationship is destined for the altar. At what point, then, should these two people be allowed to actually meet? Will they be introduced at childhood or a scant 10 minutes before the formal ceremony? What other influences will impact the anticipation/dread of that meeting? Will they be kept in the dark about the arrangement and (1) fall in love with each other on their own or (2) resent having a life partner not of their personal choosing?

The journey that your script takes follows the very same path, the difference being that the audience members themselves have been designated the "other half" in an arrangement which you, the author, have decreed. Do you want them to meet your main character as a young girl and move through the scenes as she evolves into a stunning beauty whom they can't help but fall madly in love with by the final credits?

Or is their first sight of her going to be in a dark alley where she's standing over a murder victim and whistling "Que Sera Sera?" Certainly the latter would give them plenty of pause to wonder what, exactly, they had just gotten themselves into when they committed themselves to walking into this movie to begin with.

Starting your story in the right place is based on an appreciation of how the different variations of "time as a template" can significantly affect the structure and complexity of the same story. If the method you're using on your current script keeps resulting in mental cul-de-sacs, a different approach may be just the ticket you need to greenlight the plot and get it past page 1.

LINEAR

The most often-used formula of storytelling is "linear time." In linear time, as in real life, events happen chronologically. Example: Walter wakes up on a Thursday, eats his breakfast, catches the Metro, heads toward his office, and finds an antique brass lamp tucked in the bottom drawer of his desk that wasn't there the day before.

Where would you start this movie?

Certainly the hook/leading question involves the mysterious appearance of the brass lamp. Since the plot presumably revolves around Walter's unexpected discovery, it would seem logical to introduce that discovery as early as possible. On the other hand, showing that Walter's life has been pretty routine and boring up until the time he opens his drawer helps to establish a "before and after" contrast.

Whether the lamp (1) has magical powers, (2) is stolen loot that was stashed for safekeeping, or (3) is a gift from a secret admirer in the typing pool, Walter's life will not be the same at the end of the film as it was when the film began. The trick with linear storytelling is determining just how much "pre-story" an audience really needs in order to understand the main event.

BOOKENDS

In the "bookend" method of storycrafting, the bulk of the plot is told in the form of one big flashback. James Cameron's *Titanic* is an easy example of how this works. At the beginning of the movie, we meet the elderly Rose in conjunction with the salvage operations of the famous ship. The middle of this movie focuses on all of the past events leading up to and including its collision with the iceberg. The film concludes in the present with elderly Rose. Even though we are familiar with the oceanliner's real-life fate with destiny, what we don't know are all of the individual stories of heroism and cowardice among the characters on board.

Likewise, *Little Big Man*, starring Dustin Hoffman, employed the same technique of storytelling by having the incidents pertinent to Custer's Last Stand revolve around its only survivor, Jack Crabb. Plausibility is inherent in both of these fictitious personas because of our frame of reference regarding the kind of people who, respectively, booked passage to a new world and those who chose to redefine what they felt their current world should be.

Had either story started anywhere other than where it did, we would not have been swept up in wanting to learn how these characters of advanced age managed to endure the same circumstances where so many others had perished. We identify with them not because of the events themselves but because of the emotional chords they pluck in striving to rise above changes that are beyond their control.

The biggest disadvantage with bookends, of course (and especially in stories regarding pulse-pounding adventure), is that no matter what the danger is, we still know for a fact that the lead character lived to tell about it.

Let's apply this to the story of Walter and the brass lamp. In a bookend version, Walter is now a grandfather living a comfortable life in a mansion in Kentucky. His grandchildren come to play and ride his horses. One of them picks the brass lamp off a shelf and is instantly warned by Grandpa Walter that the lamp has dangerous powers. We then flashback to the past to learn exactly what those powers are and how Walter himself came to be a wealthy man. Was it because of the lamp or in spite of it? Inquiring minds want to know.

PARALLEL TIME

In 1998, Gwyneth Paltrow starred in *Sliding Doors*, a story in which her character's life is played out in two parallel dimensions which split off from the initial premise of catching or missing a certain train. How a seemingly random incident such as this can result in two entirely different outcomes for the heroine is a good example of the concept of parallel time. Mystery stories are another popular place where this method is used; for instance, showing what each of the various suspects was doing during the very same timeframe.

Parallel universe storytelling can be complicated to carry off effectively but does offer many intriguing possibilities. Let's say that we try this with a Good Walter/Bad Walter scenario. The Good Walter finds the lamp, discovers its enchanted properties, and uses his wishes to benefit his friends and community. The Bad Walter, however, uses the same lamp's powers to get rich, get girlfriends, and get back at other people.

This is a wonderful exercise for exploring morality issues and pointing up the consequences of selfish actions. At the end of the Good Walter story, his self-lessness and compassion reap their own reward in terms of recognition and happiness. The Bad Walter, however, brings only ruin and misery upon himself.

THE MAYPOLE

The most complex device for storytelling has already been given several names: serpentine, spiral, wraparound, and corkscrew. "Maypole," however, is my own term for it and conjures the English image of a tall pole with colorful streamers, around which merrymakers frolic. Their respective proximity to the pole itself depends on how many times they circle it and whether it's always in the same direction. In a maypole fashion of plot development, there are multiple flashbacks and multiple points of view, each revolving around one central event, object or theme.

Kenneth Branagh's 1991 *Dead Again* is an example of this convoluted technique

The central issue of a murder in the past and an amnesiac woman in the present (Emma Thompson) is coupled with a theme of reincarnation that alludes to the notion that we continue to encounter the same people throughout multiple lifetimes.

Let's say that in the Walter story, the maypole is the lamp itself and that Walter is not its first owner. The plot then weaves back and forth among the prior owners, incorporating flashbacks and futuristic sequences of what actually happened to them and what they wanted to have happen, instead. Maypoles are very tricky to handle well. Why? Because if you don't know where your characters are at all times and what they're doing, they could literally collide and tie themselves into knots!

REVERSE ENGINEERING

If you *really* want to mess with an audience's collective mind, of course, you can try something along the lines of *Memento* or the episode of television's *Seinfeld* in which the character of Elaine recounts a wedding in India from the present backwards. Using the aforementioned Walter scenario, the story would begin with the end product of Walter's use of the lamp and work its way back to the original discovery of the lamp in the bottom drawer of his desk.

TIME AS YOU KNOW IT

> Identify three films that utilize the linear formula:

$$A > B$$

> Identify three films that utilize the bookend formula:

$$B > A > B$$

> Identify three films that utilize the parallel formula:

$$A > \left\{ \begin{array}{c} B > C > D \\ E > F > G \end{array} \right\} > H$$

> Identify three films that utilize the maypole formula:

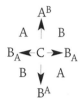

> Identify three films that do not use any of the above formulas.
> What type of linear or non-linear progression works best for your film idea? Why?

Now that you know which time formula best fits your movie plot, it's time to divvy up the action. In order to do that, however, you need to be aware of the pitfalls inherent in the traditional three-act format.

AMBITIOUS OPENINGS

A common problem I see with novice screenwriters is a failure to recognize when they've done enough introductions and need to move on. The enthusiasm to start a new story and bring the audience on board often results in a front-loaded script that is too heavy on character detail and exposition to successfully propel itself forward. The longer it takes to get the conflict underway, the less time you will have remaining to resolve it.

SAGGING MIDDLES

Have you ever started something with great zeal and run out of steam about halfway through? Maybe it's a result of external distractions. Maybe it's the fact that where you thought you wanted to go with the plot just didn't work out the way you envisioned. Yet another scenario is that you hadn't prepared a preliminary outline and now have no idea what's supposed to transpire next. Think of your plot as a wet bedsheet; if you only had two clothespins to hang it up, where's it going to sag?

SLAP-DASH FINALES

Yikes! You just finished page 115 of your murder mystery screenplay and the inspector still hasn't figured out who the killer is. Time for drastic measures. You promptly assemble all the usual suspects in a parlor and — wow, what a surprise — have the protagonist explain everything in dialogue that you ran out of time to reveal through action. Or perhaps you decide to endow your super-hero with amazing abilities he didn't previously possess in order to extricate him from a perilous fate. Such contrivances reflect that, somewhere along the path, the writer became more interested in finishing the script than in providing a satisfying pay-off.

FOUR-PART HARMONY

In order to address these scripting conundrums, my own approach employs a four-act template which can be applied to any genre, any length, and any medium.

It starts out with an 8-1/2 x 11 inch piece of paper.

The first thing you need to do is turn the paper sideways to a landscape mode and fold it vertically into four equal columns. At the top of the first column, write the words: FORESHADOWING – 1ST 10 MINUTES. At the bottom of the last column, write the words: UH-OH—LAST 10 MINUTES. Leave a space below each of these notations; we'll get back to them later on.

How this template works is that you divide the total length of your project by four. If you are writing a two-hour film, for example, each column represents a 30-minute increment. This method also applies to page-count and chapter manuscripts; i.e., if you're writing a novel and want it to be 24 chapters, each column would address 6 of them.

Before you start writing your screenplay, you are going to jot down an equal number of key actions that occur in each block and which escalate the central conflict.

THE TEMPLATE

ACT ONE	ACT TWO	ACT THREE	ACT FOUR
FIRST TEN MINUTES			LAST TEN MINUTES

*

**

* Foreshadowing

** Uh-Oh

Let's start with a really simple one.

> Column 1 – Boy meets girl and falls in love.
> Column 2 – Boy loses girl.
> Column 3 – Girl gets engaged to someone else.
> Column 4 – Wedding is scheduled to take place.

From the looks of it, it appears that our hero is doomed to lose his lady love. But wait! As the clock ticks down to the exchange of wedding vows, our hero suddenly remembers something that is going to change the whole equation. This is called the "Uh-oh" and is tied back to whatever foreshadowing was introduced in the first act. In this case, the hero was at the airport heading back to Los Angeles after a business trip and casually witnessed a man being welcomed home by his wife and three young children. This scene comes early enough in the film that most of the audience will quickly forget about it.

We're now in the fourth act when the hero has reluctantly decided to show his support for the bride by coming to the ceremony. Keep in mind that, up until this point, he has never seen the groom who robbed him of a happily ever after. As she starts down the aisle, he suddenly can't shake the feeling that he knows this guy from somewhere.

Uh-oh! It's that same guy he saw two months ago at Heathrow. Just in the nick of time, he speaks up, stops the wedding from proceeding, and just might possibly manage to win his lady love back by the closing credits.

As you get accustomed to using this template each time you outline a new film idea, you'll find it much easier to equitably distribute the action and allow a reasonable amount of time for each significant plot point to develop. The template can also be set up and saved as an Excel chart on your computer.

WHEN TIME PERMITS

To see how this template works with existing films, watch a few movies or television shows with a stopwatch and log the critical plot points throughout. What you'll discover is that the conflict escalates in balanced proportions throughout the entire script, regardless of its length.

CHAPTER 8 | BEEN THERE, DONE THAT

If you were going to build a house, you wouldn't just nail a couple boards together on a vacant lot and throw a tarp on top for a roof. You'd want to find the best location, secure the proper permits, learn everything you could about architecture and construction, buy quality materials, hire experts to assist with the tricky parts, and stick to a workable schedule so that your new dwelling could be completed while you still had plenty of years to enjoy it.

Unfortunately, a lot of beginning writers ignore this useful analogy when it comes to building a script from the ground up. They throw together a flimsy framework, refuse to seek out advice on how it could be improved, and abandon it after the first deluge of rejections.

In order to write for the movies, you not only need to understand movies from the inside out but invest in the necessary research to make your plot ring true, regardless of the locale, the era, or the livelihoods of the characters who people it.

HAVE WE SEEN THIS BEFORE?
A Web site that merits special mention is the Internet Movie Database at *www.imdb.com*. Its applicability to this chapter is that you can conduct searches on titles, characters, and even plots to determine if someone else has beaten you to the punch.

Let's say, for example, that you want to write a screenplay about Madame Curie. If you type in the words "Madame Curie" under the "Character" search, it will reveal that 10 prior films had characters by that name appearing in them. Or let's say you want to do a search on "Ninjas." Twenty-five Ninja-themed movies will be provided for you. On even broader categories such as "World War II," the search under the "Plots" link will yield hundreds of entries, attesting to the popularity of this theme. By linking to each of the named films in a given category, you can see how previous screenwriters handled the same subject matter.

You can even do an inquiry related to specific movie titles. Although stand-alone titles do not fall under the same copyright laws as full manuscripts, it's helpful to find out whether someone has already grabbed up *Overboard* before you decide to use it yourself and/or whether its plot covers similar ground and characters.

BEST OF THE BEST

Certainly the highest praise an author can hear are the words, "This is the best thing I've ever read!" If you want a scriptreader to make the same proclamation, it helps to know what Hollywood considers to be the cream of the cinema crop. Look no farther than the Web site of the American Film Institute located at *www.afi.com*.

You've probably heard a lot about AFI's "best" lists but hadn't considered until now how its contents are applicable to your ongoing film education. Each year, this organization publishes 100 titles/names of what/who the industry considers to be representative of Hollywood's best work. These decisions are based on a variety of criteria and have included such categories as "100 Best Movies," "100 Best Heroes and Villains," "100 Best Love Stories," etc.

While you're as certain to discover that some of your personal faves don't make the list as you're likely to be puzzled by some of those that do, it's a good place to start, as far as deciding what videos to rent as study guides. Let's say, for instance, that your quest is to write passionate love stories. The top three films on AFI's list of "Passions" are *Casablanca, Gone With the Wind,* and *West Side Story.*

> What are the obstacles facing the lovers in each of these films?
> How does the environment impact the circumstances of their attraction?
> Do the respective couples live happily ever after?
> What makes these three romances memorable for audiences?
> What elements does your movie love story have in common with these three classics?

Another good place to assess cinema trends and popularity is the previously cited Internet Movie Database (*www.imdb.com*), one of the most comprehensive electronic sources of movie facts and trivia currently available. At the beginning of each week, statistics are posted that provide a running list of who's on top at the box office in the U.S. and the U.K. This site also includes a link (*www.imdb.com/Top/*) to the Top Films by Genre, the Top Films by Decade, and the Top Best and Worst Films of All Time.

In my screenwriting classes for both teens and adults, a favorite assignment is to take the top three movies of any given year, identify the key element of each one, and compose a synopsis that combines all three into one plot. As of the writing of this chapter, for instance, the top three contenders of 2003 are *Finding Nemo*, *Pirates of the Caribbean: The Curse of the Black Pearl*, and *The Matrix Reloaded*. Just for fun, take a moment and see what you can come up with.

WHAT YOU CAN LEARN FROM FILM REVIEWS

The pen is mightier than the sword, especially when it comes to the way that critics can slash a new film to shreds. As someone who will eventually enter this vicious arena, you need to remember that there are no educational or professional requirements involved in being a movie reviewer. All that one needs to have is an opinion and a public forum in which to share it.

For critics at hometown newspapers, for instance, what comes out in print often has very little to do with what was up on the screen. The remarks can be a factor of the weather, a predisposition toward certain actors, a bad meal after the show, a bad date after the show, or even whether they had to buy their own tickets. In a town like Sacramento, California, which used to have two rival newspapers, it was even an unspoken rule that whatever the Republican-oriented press lauded as great had to be automatically dissed by its Democratic opponent.

If you're going to study reviews as a way to learn what kind of things critics scrutinize, you need to look beyond your local gazettes. You also need to look at more than one opinion and separate those which focus on the acting and production aspects (which a writer can't control) and those which dissect and analyze the story (which he or she created).

The Movie Review Query Engine ("MRQE") at www.mrqe.com is a user-friendly source not only for current box office fare but vintage films, as well. In addition, news and views can be found at:

> *www.rottentomatoes.com*
> *www.moviefone.com*
> *www.film.com*
> *www.badmovies.org*

If it's an entertaining read you're looking for, you can't beat Roger Ebert's annual collections of film criticisms available at major bookstores or through Amazon.com. Whenever I'm writing a new scene, in fact, my husband enjoys playing devil's advocate by asking, "What do you think Roger Ebert would say about this?" Even when this popular Chicago critic is totally condemning a film, it's to his credit that he does so with such mirth and finesse that you can't help but smile.

Ebert's work is also where you'll find his humorous compendium of movie clichés, among them: (1) the observation that every hotel room in France has a view of the Eiffel Tower; (2) the first time we see a movie bartender, he is wiping out a glass with a rag; and (3) anyone who ever excuses his phlegm with the remark, "oh, it's nothing, just a little cough," will die before the final credits.

LINE BY LINE
To really understand how films are put together, of course, you need to make a practice of reading as many of them as possible. Fortunately, the Internet accommodates this with a number of sites where complete screenplays and transcripts can be downloaded for free or purchased at minimum cost.

If you're planning to use these materials as a study guide for proper format, however, be aware that there is a difference between an actual script and a transcription.

A script will look just like a script is supposed to but it's not necessarily the same version as the one actually produced. There also will be incarnations that include numbered scenes, something which would not be used in screenplays you submit for consideration. Watching the film while you're holding a copy of the downloaded script is one of the best ways to really appreciate the correlation between the written word and the cinema image. If you're someone who's inclined to use excessive verbiage, you'll be surprised by just how little is actually written to convey a big idea.

A transcription is exactly what it implies; someone has watched the entire film or TV episode and meticulously documented everything that was said or done. While the dialogue or action will be verbatim in a transcription edition, it will bear little resemblance to a correctly formatted screenplay or teleplay and, therefore, should not be regarded as an accurate model.

Here's where you can find hundreds of scripts to download or purchase:

> *www.simplyscripts.com*
> *www.scriptdude.com*
> *www.harvestmoon.com*
> *www.geocities.com/tvtranscripts/*
> *www.13idol.com/store/scriptsmain.html*
> *www.script-o-rama.com/tv/tvscript.shtml*
> *www.scriptfly.com*

BOOKS

For those of you who like to add books to your library, clearinghouses such as Writer's Digest Books often include hardcover and paperback editions of popular TV series such as *The West Wing* and *Frasier*, as well as complete scripts for screenplays such as *Shakespeare In Love* and *Casablanca*. In addition to the scripts themselves, you'll find a variety of development notes, stills, and interviews.

WHAT'S THE COMPETITION UP TO?

Several years back, Francis Ford Coppola launched an innovative film site called Zoetrope (*www.zoetrope.com*) on which screenwriters could give and receive feedback on each other's scripts. How it works is that you upload one of your scripts to their system, then read four scripts by other writers who have already posted. As soon as your critiques are completed, you receive comments from everyone who has read *your* script.

One of the benefits my clients are all in agreement about is that reading the work of their peers helps them to sharpen their own skills. An example of this was a young man who noticed that the author of a script he selected had a fondness for starting every other line of dialogue with "Well." When he later went back to edit one of his own projects, he discovered that he was guilty — though to a lesser extent — of the very same habit.

A PESKY LITTLE DETAIL CALLED ACCURACY

In addition to making your screenplay as bulletproof as possible in terms of presentation, you also need to be sure that the actual content is accurate. With the number of on-ramps available to today's information highway, there's simply no excuse for sloppy guesswork. Online encyclopedias, reference books, and bonafide experts will be your most valuable friends as you traverse new territory in your plots.

Nowhere are these professional assists more needed, of course, than in defining what, exactly, your fictional characters do for a living.

In the contemporary screenplays I review, the three most common occupations depicted are:

> > Advertising/public relations executives
> > Detectives
> > Hookers

Unfortunately, they are also replete with all of the traits that are straight from Cliches 'R' Us. Specifically, the ad executives work "normal" hours and have an inordinate amount of leisure time on their hands, the detectives conduct amateurish investigations in between drinking and spontaneous sex, and the hookers — yes, you guessed it — they have hearts of gold.

While movie magic can grant us certain leaps of logic (i.e., even the lowest paid waitress in the story lives in a bigger NYC apartment than the rest of us could ever afford), your chances for a sale will rapidly disappear if the dialogue, action, and supposed facts are rampantly inconsistent with reality. If you're unfamiliar with the lingo of Wall Street wizards or drawing a blank on what constitutes a prison warden's day, don't write a single scene until you've done your homework and brushed up on what the "been there/done that" pros have to say.

Three of the most fun sources to get you started on the path of "career accuracy" in your storyline are:

> Surfing for
Slang*www.spraakservice.net/slangportal/*
A link that you can access from the *www.1000dictionaries.com*
Web site, this comprehensive resource covers American,
British, Irish, Australian, and a host of other national slangs,
as well as the jargon associated with gangsters, drug lords,
gays and lesbians, law enforcement, etc.

> *The Crime Writer's Reference Guide: 1001 Tips for Writing
the Perfect Murder* by Martin Roth (Michael Wiese
Productions).

> Writer's Digest "Howdunit Series"
This innovative collection shows you the ropes on everything
your characters need to know to commit a crime... or to solve
one. Some of the titles include:*Murder One: A Writer's
Guide to Homicide;Armed and Dangerous: A Writer's Guide
to Weapons; Just the Facts, Ma'am: A Writer's Guide to
Investigators and Investigation Techniques;Deadly Does: A*

Writer's Guide to Poisons. Not only do they provide an accurate overview for crime and mystery screenwriters, but they also contribute to startled reactions by one's dinner guests if accidentally left out on a coffee table.

> *Careers for Your Characters: A Writer's Guide to 101 Professions from Architect to Zookeeper.* (By Raymond Obstfeld and Frank Neumann, Writer's Digest Books, 2001). This text provides descriptions of job duties, salaries, buzz words, wardrobes, and tools of the trade. It also lists book, film, and television titles where these professions are highlighted.

CHAPTER 9 | ARE YOU A SOLO ACT, A DUET, OR JUST THE MESSENGER?

Dear Ms. Hamlett:

I came up with an idea that everyone says would make a great movie. I don't know anything about how to write a script so I was thinking I could give it to you since you're a successful writer and we could split everything 50/50 when you sell it for me.

At least half a dozen times a month, I can count on receiving variations of this generous invitation. Each one, of course, gets the same response, carefully couched in terms that are more diplomatic than what I'd *really* like to say; specifically, "Do you think I'm an idiot or what?"

Over the years, I've also discovered that I'm not the only one sought out by coat-tail novices. Fellow novelists, playwrights, and even an advice columnist ("I could fill in for you until I get syndicated myself") are regularly approached to help ghostwrite the future of total strangers. While I think some of them really believe that a gutsy approach will impress the target reader as the sign of a zealous entrepreneur, the majority really don't know any better and are somehow convinced they are doing us a favor by volunteering free ideas in the context of their companionship.

Reality check: People who are successful writers got that way by devoting time and energy to their *own* ideas. While it's one thing to give advice and be a mentor to newbies, the prospect of doing virtually all the work for half the pay and recognition just isn't one that a professional author is going to pounce on with glee any time soon.

That's not to say, of course, your stellar plot will never see the light of day. There are actually four viable options open to you, any one of which can help get your story where you want it to be.

WRITE IT AS SOMETHING ELSE FIRST

In the chapter on stage, page or cinema, you learned how different aspects of a story are handled, depending on the chosen medium. If your plot is one that could potentially work in a venue other than film, you may want to explore writing it as such before you try your hand at a screenplay.

This method accomplishes three things.

The first is that it commits you to a pattern of discipline and forces you to complete whatever bright idea you have initiated. Writing — any kind of writing — is hard work. Certainly the attraction of a collaborative effort is that you would seemingly have to do a lot less. This craft, however, is one that is predicated on passion. In order to understand that passion, you need to immerse yourself in it as deeply as possible. Simply passing off an idea to someone else while you go to the mall isn't going to wed you to your characters or to any of the conflict in which they are engaged.

The second benefit of writing your idea as something else first is that it will reveal if you actually *have* a full-fledged story to tell. Many a time I've had a student start out with a promising enough premise, only to look bewildered when I queried what was going to happen next. "I hadn't really thought the rest of it through," they reply. "I was kinda hoping *you* could tell me."

The third advantage of this practice relates to the possibility of the short story, novel, or stage play getting published or winning a prize in competition. What better way to start out an inquiry letter to a prospective buyer than to share that someone else has recognized its merit and excellence.

HANDING IT OFF

Over the years, I've known a number of individuals who view themselves as "idea factories." With neither the interest nor skill level to develop any projects themselves, they've been more than happy to share their concepts with anyone who wants to write them. Perhaps you fit that model yourself — someone who would just like a particular story to get made but doesn't necessarily want or need to be part of the process.

You might want to start out with people in your immediate circle. Are there screenwriters in your family or social community to whom you'd feel comfortable pitching the idea? Maybe you're taking classes at the local university and there are fellow students looking for hot ideas they'd like to turn into scripts.

The Internet offers further opportunities for finding writers to take your idea and run with it. If you've never visited "Craig's List" before (*www.craigslist.com*), this would be a good time to add it to your bookmarks. Not only will you find regional opportunity listings but the film-related links often include posts by aspiring screenwriters or start-up production companies seeking original concepts for development.

Keep in mind, however, that giving your storyline away to someone else means that you are also relinquishing control of what they actually do with it. And, unless you've delineated specific terms in a contract, you can't come back after the picture has been turned into a gazillion dollar success and claim that they stole it from you.

TACKLING IT YOURSELF

One of my recent e-mail inquiries was from a man who had acquired the rights to a human interest story that had made the headlines in his hometown. "I don't know the first thing about how to write a movie," he explained, "but a venture capitalist in Arizona said he'd help me raise five million dollars to start my own production company and film it. What do you think I should do?"

My initial reaction, of course, is that the venture capitalist's name is probably Guido and that he is more interested in the prospective company failing than he is in bettering the filmmaking community by giving this new kid a chance at playing producer. My recommendation was that the writer buy some screenwriting books, take some classes, and do the first draft himself.

There is certainly no shortage of helpful advice that is out there for beginners, far more than was ever in place when I first began writing movie and play reviews in the early 70s and testing the magazine markets with a few fillers. Since the Internet hadn't been invented yet, we were the generation who learned just about everything from trial and error — relying on reference books that were already obsolete by the time they got to the printers, spending copious amounts on postage, spending even more copious amounts of time at the mailbox waiting for our SASEs to find their way home.

We were also of the generation who believed that you absolutely had to move to Los Angeles if you ever wanted to crack the system and be a part of it. While it certainly doesn't hurt to have a Southern Cal address, technology has made it possible for people who live in the hinterlands of Maine to still get their work into the right hands... and get it produced.

Bottom line: whatever excuse you might fashion on why you can't try writing a screenplay on your own is probably not going to wash.

"But what if I try to write it and it doesn't sell?" the man wrote back. "I'd feel miserable for having failed."

Failure, I reminded him, is when you never take the chance at all.

ONLINE LEARNING

Want to dabble in a screenwriting class to see if you have an aptitude for it but don't have the time and money to devote to a university semester or a summer film camp? Online or "distance learning" classes enable you to work at your own pace, participate in chat room discussions, and get feedback on your progress. Here's a sample of what's available for cyberspace students:

> *Scr(i)pt Magazine*
www.scriptmag.com/pages/classestoc.shtml

> Writer on Line
www.writeronline.us

> Screenwriters' Utopia
www.screenwritersutopia.com

> Charles Deemer
www.screenwrights.com

PARTNERS IN RHYME

One of the great joys I derive from collaborating on theater musicals is that I never know what it will sound like until the composers send me tapes. Unlike Rodgers and Hammerstein, who probably spent more time in the same room with each other than they did with their families, our own brainstorming process is accomplished by phone, e-mail, and the U.S. Postal Service.

Unusual? Not when you consider that our respective areas of expertise don't require any interaction in person. I don't know how to write an orchestral score. Likewise, they don't know how to write a script. We also each believe the partners really have all the talent and we're just lucky to get to work with them.

Two of my three composers came about as the result of a nationwide search. Not only were their orchestrations singable, but their accompanying letters projected humor, warmth, and focus. The third, I literally walked in on by accident on a stage in Lyndon, Vermont. Arriving early to give a speech on screenwriting, I was drawn in by the sound of someone playing original compositions on the stage piano. I liked what I heard and a mutually beneficial partnership was born on the spot.

That same level of bliss, however, cannot be said of the times I've paired with aspiring writers. It always sounds like a good idea at the start, given the solitary nature of the craft itself. Maybe you've even been considering it as a way to divide the workload and brainstorm how each scene should come together. Before you commit to a buddy system, however, the following scenarios reveal what you could be getting yourself into.

I THOUGHT I WAS JUST HERE TO WATCH

The e-mail came from out of the blue. Ten years prior, I had made the acquaintance of a women who said she had always wanted to break into writing romance novels. "Maybe we could write one together one day," she chirpily proposed. "I have lots of ideas."

I diplomatically dissuaded her, suggested she should try writing them herself.

Time passed.

When she finally resurfaced, she still hadn't written anything yet, but had been following my career. Her liberal praise — to the point of gushiness — put me on guard that she probably wanted something. She did. She wanted to write a book with me about her experience of being widowed twice in a lifetime.

Against my better judgment, I said yes, deeming that the book could be cathartic for her and inspirational to other women in the same situation. I proceeded to outline a gameplan whereby we'd interview clergy, doctors, and grief counselors, in addition to those who had suffered loss and wanted to share their experiences.

Two months into the process, I asked her how her portion of the writing was going. "Oh, I'm just here to watch you and see how it's done," she replied. What she *had* accomplished, however, was going to Nordstrom and picking out the suit she was going to wear at our first book-signing. "Do you want me to pick out something matching for you?" she offered.

> WARNING: There's nothing wrong with giving tips to new kids. Just make sure that if you take them under your wing, they don't cause both of you to fall out of the tree. Delineate what portions each partner will be responsible for and schedule progress checks to ensure that the work is being completed.

LOVE ME, LOVE MY EGO
As a result of one of my screenwriting columns, a self-published author approached me with the idea that her book would make a great film. She asked if I knew any screenwriters. I offered to read it first and render my opinion on its adaptation potential.

"I think it would make a better play," I remarked, owing largely to the fact that it was a series of humorous vignettes rather than a single, cohesive plot-line.

"Do you know any playwrights?" she asked.

By this time, we had become e-mail pen pals and I opted to develop her book into a three-act comedy for a 50/50 split of the profits.

Big mistake.

Every day, I would receive no less than two dozen e-mails telling me what I should be putting into the production. Furthermore, she was vexed with those incidents and characters I felt were expendable and, thus, omitted from the script. "Were you there?" she harangued. "How would *you* know whether or not they were important?"

Small wonder it took me nearly seven months just to write the first act. It was 45 pages — very tight, very funny, very nostalgic.

"I just have a few notes," she remarked when I sent it off to her. These "few notes" encompassed 48 pages, longer than the first act of the play itself.

"Oh and by the way," she added, "do you really think that 50/50 is really fair? Considering that you wouldn't have a story if I hadn't lived it, I think I should get 90% and you should have 10." In retrospect, I'm fairly certain that if our arrangement had continued and the play ever want on to win an award, I would have been summarily pushed off the stage and credited — if at all — as just the typist.

> WARNING: Always trust your intuition. If your potential screen partners are controlling and calling all the shots at the beginning, they will only get worse with the passage of time. It's also wise to put all of the financial particulars in a formal contract, even if the party of the first part is as sweet as your grandmother.

BUDS AND BREWSKIES

"So what exactly are you looking for in a writing partner?" I inquired. It seemed strange that someone who had already written and produced some direct-to-video projects on his own needed to suddenly bring in a partner. If, for instance, he felt he was weak on dialogue or wanted to bring in an expert on a particular era or lifestyle, a liaison would make sense.

"I'd just like a bud to kinda hang out with and shoot the bull," he said.

Wisely, I declined.

> WARNING: It's one thing if your writing partner (1) eventually becomes your best pal or (2) was your best pal before the partnership began. Seeking out or joining a partnership for the express purpose of keeping you company and splitting a beer tab could leave you worse off than if you'd remained alone. In an ideal partnership, each half should be able to supply a skill, knowledge, or connection that the other half was missing.

OUTA MY WAY!

My husband and I had yet to move from Northern California when I met a prospective writing partner who ended up teaching me the most valuable lesson about choosing collaborators.

She already lived in L.A. and was looking to break into screenwriting by adapting romance novels. Since I had several of the latter and was beginning to recognize the need to either start commuting southward or find an associate I could trust, it seemed like a good idea for us to work together.

Her zeal for schmoozing at industry parties and events soon thereafter yielded a potentially valuable contact for us. Unfortunately, the producer was only in the market for scripts featuring women over the age of 45. Rather than add an obviously contrived 20 years to our current heroine, we politely declined. Not a week later, one of my screenwriting students turned in a proposal for a film that would have been perfect. I suggested to my associate that, since she had personally met the producer, perhaps she could do a favor and play intermediary.

Her response was curt, as well as myopic.

"I'm a struggling writer myself," she declared. "I'm not about to start helping the competition beat me out of the chance to get noticed."

Like the proverbial dog in the manger, she was adamant about denying someone else access to a forum which we ourselves were unable to join at the present time. The result? The producer lost a first-rate script, the writer lost a golden opportunity, and the associate lost my respect. Rather than agree to disagree on the concept of shared resources, she punctuated the end of the relationship with the declaration that she could reach her goal entirely on her own, notwithstanding that six months earlier she had vigorously campaigned to hitch her star to mine.

On the one hand, I can relate to some of her trepidation. On the other, it's a sad commentary that we've so lost sight of faith in our fellow man that we'd purposely withhold resources that could ultimately benefit the literary community at large.

> WARNING: It's only a matter of time that a collaborator who views all other writers as the "enemy" will eventually label you in the same way. Life is too short not to hold the door open for our competitors... and I'm not referring to elevator shafts when I say that.

IF YOU'RE GOING TO WORK TOGETHER

In most of life's big events, there are those who lead and those who follow. In collaborative projects, however, this rule doesn't always work. In fact, it can be injurious to the health of the friendship if there's any kind of grapple for power to be the boss. There needs to be respect for each other's area of expertise in order to keep the partners on equal footing in contributing to a project's development.

In the case of collaborating on a book, for example, one partner may have a better handle on narrative while the other's specialty is snappy dialogue. There are even some partnerships where one person does all of the historical research and the other does the actual writing, yet both share 50/50 credits on the finished product.

With screenwriting, the division of labor might be based on physical location (i.e., the one who lives in Los Angeles or New York is responsible for pitching and "doing meetings"). Is your partner better at writing synopses and treatments? Do you have the better voice or charismatic personality on the phone for setting up appointments? Capitalize on your respective strengths. And don't get in each other's way!

ARE WRITTEN CONTRACTS NECESSARY?

The presence of a legal agreement doesn't guarantee a smooth-running partnership, any more than the hiring of an agent solidifies one's place in the literary world. In my own collaborations, I've always tried to answer the question, "Would I believe in this person as a friend even if we weren't working together?"

Unfortunately, in our lawsuit-driven society, intuition isn't enough to hold up in court in the event that (1) you and your partner come to a parting of the ways, (2) you experience "creative differences" halfway through the project's completion, or (3) one of you dies and your mourners suddenly have an attack of greed.

As starry-eyed as many people approach the benefits of collaborating (there's an obvious correlation to pre-nups and marriage vows), it's only prudent to consider what your legal options will be if you ever come to loggerheads. For the legally impaired, there's a comprehensive guidebook by Writer's Digest titled *How to Write with a Collaborator* (published in 1988). This book includes sample contract agreements in the appendix and also addresses issues such as compatibility, soliciting experts, ghostwriting, and defining respective duties. You can even find sample contracts online that allow you to fill in the blanks and print out copies for both of you. Another excellent resource is Claudia Johnson and Matt Stevens' book, *Script Partners: What Makes Film and TV Writing Teams Work* (Michael Wiese Productions).

By outlining who's in charge of what, what the percentages will be, and how the property will be marketed will save major headaches (and potential lawsuits) down the road. It's also wise to include a clause pertaining to the property's ownership should one of the partners get run over by a bus (It does happen, you know), or if one of you decides to adapt the sold/unsold script to a novel or Broadway musical and the other is lukewarm to the idea.

WHAT ARE WE TRYING TO SAY HERE?

If you're going to create something wonderful with a writing partner, it really helps if both of you are in accord on what that something is supposed to be. Sounds obvious, of course, but I can recall one of my earlier theatrical collaboration disasters when a composer and I were not only on different planes, but probably different planets.

While the musician had the creative skills and professionalism to turn out a first-rate score, we hit an immediate impasse at his interpretation of the script's intent. The musical, *First Ladies*, was based on the premise of four former presidential wives stepping out of their portraits to offer advice and counsel to an incoming First Lady. Such diversity was reflected through the "ghosts" of Martha Washington, Dolly Madison, Rachel Jackson, and Mary Lincoln.

"The concept's passable," the musician remarked with an unabashed yawn, "but I'd rather spin something with Eleanor, Mamie, Nancy and Roslyn."

"I'll get back to you," I replied. I didn't.

A similar incident occurred when two of my students decided to team up on a movie of the week which was set in the Pacific Northwest and involved park rangers. After two weeks of intense writing, it became apparent that one of them was writing a love story while the other one was penning a sensational murder mystery. They came running to me to mediate, each convinced that her own way of telling the story was better.

"She wants to kill off Bradley in the first scene," the romantic argued.

"That's 'cause her 'Bradley' character is an idiot," her partner countered, not realizing that Bradley was supposed to be the heroine's heartthrob and, thus, meant to last for more than the first chapter.

TRY TO KEEP UP WITH ME

If you're going to work together, it's important that you and your partner(s) not only march to the same drummer, but also at the same pace. Several people who responded to my ad for a collaborator took nearly a year to send a sample of their work. The message conveyed to me was that either it had taken them that long to assemble their best material or that they were too lazy about finding a postage stamp.

Promising as some of the pieces were (when they finally arrived), my decision to ultimately pass on them stemmed from the experience of getting frustrated with delays that aren't of my own making. If, for instance, it takes someone two weeks to write one scene and it takes the partner over three months to respond with the subsequent scene, it will either takes years for them to finish anything cohesive... or no time at all to end the friendship.

If and when you *do* find someone with whom to write a film, approach the project just as you'd approach an assignment at work; specifically, by determining intermediate deadlines for completion of each component. While it's true that some people work better under pressure and like to wait until zero hour to turn anything in, it's not a practice that lends itself to working as a team.

By laying a solid foundation of understanding, a good collaboration should unite the best of all talents, a shared expectation of the result, and — last but not least — someone with whom to celebrate when the first check comes in!

CHAPTER 10 | SHOW US YOUR SPECS AND SHORTS

As a writer, you are the salesperson of your own best talent. Your screenplays — your wares — are the creative merchandise that you will be putting into circulation with the hope of stirring consumer interest and a "gotta have it" attitude. This chapter explains how expanding your story-telling repertoire through spec scripts and shorts can increase your chances of a sale... and a long-term career.

MAKING A SPECTACLE OF YOUR WRITING

Until such time as your screenplays start getting the attention and notoriety they deserve from agents, director, and producers, the bulk of what you write will be done "on spec." "Spec" is short for "speculation" and means exactly that: maybe you'll sell it, maybe you won't. (Hence, the wisdom of having a day job to keep your creditors happy in the meantime.)

Spec scripts take two forms; specifically, those that are written for an existing television series and those that are original concepts. The purpose of both is essentially the same: to provide a sample of writing that demonstrates your comfort level and expertise with a given platform or genre.

THE SMALL SCREEN

Let's say that you have been a fan of *The West Wing* since Day 1 and know President Bartlet's Oval Office staff as well as you know your own family. Furthermore, you've made a study of the program's multi-layered structure in terms of introducing new White House crises and revisiting past character foibles.

While it's not terribly likely that *TWW's* current writers are going to pull out a chair and invite you to join them for doughnuts and weekly brainstorming, a spec script that captures the show's cadence, nuances, and emotional energy will nevertheless make an impression on a prospective agent, a contest judge, or a producer looking to launch a similarly themed show regarding American political infrastructure.

It goes without saying, of course, that you need to maintain some semblance of coloring within the lines. For instance, a plot in which a high school friend of Zoey's turns out to be a hooker and puts Josh in a compromising position in the eyes of the press could be introduced and resolved within the one-hour dramatic framework. Likewise, the ensemble reaction to an incident ripped from national headlines (i.e., a nuclear accident, a high-profile crime, the assassination of a prominent foreign ally) becomes the backdrop for the characters' respective — and oftentimes predictable — displays of strength and weakness.

On the other hand, a story in which President Bartlet comes out of the closet and professes passion for a summer intern named Maurice presents an irreversible challenge that doesn't mesh with the vision of the show's originators. True, such a development would be daring, unexpected, and put Nielsen ratings through the roof. Remember, however, that your objective here is to show your perception of the show *as is*, not how you might *like* it to be just to shake up the status quo.

Another approach to spec writing for television is to take a program that is no longer on the air and either script a reunion of the core characters or simply a continuation of the last broadcast episode. What accounts for the popularity of this strategy, I think, is Hollywood's retro trend of bringing back, via feature film, the shows that baby boomers grew up with (i.e., *Lost in Space, Charlie's Angels, The Wild Wild West*). While there has certainly been plenty of evidence to support the adage that you really *can't* go home again, this scriptwriting strategy nonetheless offers more latitude in terms of program content than current, long-running hits in which the structure is more tightly defined.

There is also the avenue of submitting spec scripts for network and cable programs that have yet to build a following and, thus, may be open to what your imagination has to offer. Granted, the shows may get canceled before your episode ever airs, but you still will have had the opportunity to participate on a writing team and get valuable feedback that can be applied to your subsequent efforts.

Don't rule out teleplay competitions, either, or the opportunity to place spec TV scripts on Web sites such as *www.InkTip.com*. Again, both of these arenas are an opportunity to demonstrate your talent for creative mimicry, advancing the suggestion that if you're that skilled at copying an existing format, you're probably also adept at following the instructions of development personnel on something new. InkTip in particular (formerly Writers Script Network) has a consistently high percentage of writers who are approached to develop projects based on their handling of dialogue and pacing in hypothetical episodes of sitcoms and crime dramas.

IDEA-STARTERS

> Identify a television program (past or present) that you feel you know well enough to write a spec script for.
> What is the show's main thread of continuity that runs through every storyline? For example:

> *Gilligan's Island*
> The castaways want to get off the island.

> *7th Heaven*
> God never hands us more than we can handle.

> *Everybody Loves Raymond*
> Family: you can't live with 'em and you can't live next door to 'em.

> How does your idea interface with the core premise of the series?

> If your idea doesn't fit the chosen show's parameters, come up with a different idea OR select a different show where that idea would be compatible.

EXAMPLE: You decide to write a script that illustrates the ripple effect of unprotected sex in the transmission of HIV. As topical a subject as that is, the dramatic nature of your message wouldn't fit the castaways of the S.S. Minnow nor any members of the Romano household. It would, however, be a natural for *7th Heaven* whereby someone in the minister's congregation or community faces the deadly consequences of prior actions.

THE BIGGER PICTURE

My Aunt Liz always has been an apologist for her waffles. In spite of the fact that she has been making them for over half a decade of Sunday mornings, she continues to be dismayed every time the first one turns out badly and has to be thrown out.

An analogy can be drawn to writers and their first scripts. No matter how committed you are to making that first one come out perfect, it's more important that you jump in and give it a try than if you cautiously contemplate the process for years without ever actually doing anything about it. It's also important that you start your next one immediately thereafter and apply what you've learned on how to make it better.

This is how a portfolio of spec scripts gets built for feature films and MOWs (movies of the week). Whether your objective is to specialize in just one area such as comedy or if you want to demonstrate your range in a variety of genres, the end-product is a ready supply of samples that you can pull out at a moment's notice whenever someone asks, "Do you have something finished that I can read?"

In addition, a cache of completed scripts will also allow you to respond to the invitation, "This one didn't quite work for me but I really like your style. Do you have anything else?" If they end up having to wait six months to a year for you to come up with something, in all likelihood they will have forgotten they ever asked, necessitating a re-introduction of who, exactly, you are and why they liked you.

How many times in your life have you had to pass up an opportunity because (1) you didn't have enough gas in your car, (2) your lucky suit wasn't ironed, or (3) you hadn't set anything aside for a rainy day? The Scouting movement may have coined the motto "Be Prepared" but it's a mantra that aptly serves the writing community, as well. Those ideas in your head may be the very best plots anyone has ever come up with but until such time as a device is invented that can scan the contents of your brain directly onto paper, you still need to write them down in order for someone else to recognize their value.

So how many spec scripts constitute a good sample of what kind of writer you are? And why, for that matter, can't you just go with the singular masterpiece you really poured your heart into? Shouldn't that tell them enough about your capabilities?

Unfortunately, it's a reality of this business that you may need to write quite a few stories that you're *not* particularly wedded to in order to open doors for those projects that *are* dear. That's okay. It is through this succession of works that you'll perfect your craft and create networking opportunities that would not have been available if you only had *one* script to show for your abilities. Granted, that one script could well be a future Oscar candidate, but getting someone to finance the dream is not unlike trying to get your first credit card; everyone would love to give you one... as long as someone else takes the risk first and proves you worthy.

That said, the more amenable and versatile you are when it comes to modifying your scripts in response to advertised needs, the closer you'll get to selling the very plots that made you want to get into this career in the first place.

Not surprisingly, those projects which have interchangeable and/or generic components built into them are among the easiest to push forward on producer "Scripts Wanted" callboards such as those found at *www.hollywoodlitsales.com*, *www.backstage.com*, *www.madscreenwriter.com*, and *www.moviebytes.com*.

Take location, for instance. The more geographical specificity you introduce, the harder it is for a producer to supplant his/her own locale in that scene. Therefore, unless the setting itself is integral to the action, aim for neutrality.

For example, let's pretend you have scripted a conversation between two lobbyists that transpires in the bar of Aïoli Bodega Española in midtown Sacramento on the corner of 18th and L Streets. Now if the production company happens to operate in California's capital city, this Spanish/North African eatery is probably well known to them. But what if you submit your script to a producer in Des Moines? With nothing comparable in all of Iowa to go on, he or she might pass on a perfectly great script when all the writer had to do was describe the bar's address and attributes in less exacting terms.

The same holds true with characters, a topic which is discussed at length in Chapter 15. If the two leads in your comedy script are a pair of Latinas who run a thrift shop and you run across a script search for a comedy in which two African American girlfriends manage a book store, are you going to ignore it? Or are you going to utilize the search-and-replace feature on your computer and make the necessary tweaks to fit what the producer is seeking?

One word of caution in this exercise, of course, and that's to make sure your switcharoos aren't obvious. I am reminded of a screenplay contest I judged in which the theme of the submissions was to celebrate the quality of life found in Sacramento. One of the entrants had apparently decided that his much recycled script about a jaded gumshoe would pass muster if he simply replaced the word "Chicago" with "Sacramento" every time it appeared in the text. What he neglected to check, however, was the weather. For nearly 10 pages, his protagonist contemplated the meaning of life as he trudged through the bitter cold and "snow-choked downtown streets."

He didn't win.

RECOMMENDED READING

Writer's Guide to Places (2003) written by Jack Heffron and Don Prues. Publisher: Writer's Digest Books. This user-friendly guide gives insider tips on landmarks, eateries, demographics, social concerns, myths, and neighborhoods throughout all 50 United States and Canadian Provinces. It's not only a handy reference for when you *do* want to be specific about a story location but also for those times when you're tailoring an existing project to fit someone else's preferred locale.

WRITING SHORTS THAT WILL KNOCK THEIR SOCKS OFF

If the idea of writing a feature length screenplay as your first project sounds daunting, you may want to start out with something smaller. Many aspiring novelists, for instance, hone their narrative skills on short stories for magazines before committing to a full book. Beginning screenwriters use this strategy in creating and funding mini-samples of their work for film festivals in order to garner attention for their future, larger-scale endeavors.

Sound fun? This is where your television can become your new best friend and teach you how to use the same techniques that advertisers employ in crafting lasting impressions in a compact space of time.

In the early 1990s, Taster's Choice® launched what would become a successful series of coffee commercials that instantly stirred (no pun intended) the public's attention. The 60-second increments featured the flirtatious attraction between two strangers who live in the same apartment building and who are brought together by circumstance: one of them needs to borrow coffee from the other.

Audiences loved the concept of recurring characters whose mini love story nudged forward a few months at a time, always ending in some sort of cliffhanger. Recognizing an opportunity when they saw one, the sponsors went so far as to publicize a national writing contest (yours truly was a finalist) and offered as part of the prize package a private screening of one of the upcoming episodes. "Just don't tell your friends," they warned us after the awards dinner. "Make them wait and see." Such torture was nothing less than delicious.

This approach to marketing also was embraced by Hallmark Cards®, Country Crock Margarine®, Budweiser®, and others, providing us with entertaining station breaks that actually made us stay in the living room to see how the respective stories would come out. The only downside, of course, occurred when writers got too clever for their own good, bringing us romantic comedy commercials in which the actual product somehow got lost amidst the speculation of whether James Garner and Mariette Hartley — and later, Howie Long and Teri Hatcher — were really husband and wife.

As a communications major in college, I had been studying the dynamics of commercial ads long before I ever launched a touring theater company and began writing plays. To my surprise, the penchant I still retain for penning scripts and books with twists and "Aha!" moments derives from understanding how advertisers capture our attention through creative storytelling.

The immediate example that comes to mind was a spot done by Wells Fargo Bank in which a road-weary traveler in a century past is assisted by a teller who's working late. Appreciative of the bank employee's responsiveness in an after-hours emergency, the traveler asks if he might put in a good word for him. The teller, of course, turns out to be none other than Henry Wells himself.

This type of "revelation vein" is one that I often use in setting up audiences for a denouement that will catch them off guard. With *Exit, Grand Balcony*, for instance, they are vicariously swept up in the backstage dalliance between a married actress and one of her former leading men. When he refuses to fall in with the plans she has made to leave her husband, she pulls a gun on him, a gun which — unbeknownst to her — fits in well with his own agenda for later that evening. The name of her lover? John Wilkes Boothe.

I use commercials in my workshops as examples of the power of brevity, the ability to maximize one's allotment of space. Given the cost of advertising, especially during high-profile events such as the Super Bowl, every second of air-time has to count, calling for imagination and extremely tight wordsmithing to fit a 30- or 60-second framework.

Short films (abbreviated as "shorts") lend themselves to exactly the same dynamics and structure that PR firms use in framing a story to sell a product. Why? Because both venues are *only selling one idea* in a compressed timeframe, as opposed to multiple products or — in the case of feature-length movies — peripheral plots and themes. A short, thus, isn't simply a big story squished into a small box but, rather, a *facet* of a big story that has been momentarily isolated and magnified in order to make a point.

At the same time, a well-financed commercial spot follows exactly the same structure common to all films; specifically, even if the ad is only a minute long, a complete story with a definitive beginning, middle, and end still has to be conveyed. To simply meander without a purpose won't hook our attention, nor will it accomplish its ultimate goal of generating a sale or influencing public opinion.

For a short to click at film festivals and contests on the same level as a successful ad, there are five conditions that need to be met:
> Minimum casting
> Minimum scenes
> A Problem
> An Attempt to Resolve
> A Resolution

As an example, here's one of Budweiser's most popular commercials:

The setting is an Old West street on the back lot of a Hollywood studio. The director and camera crew are frustrated with their canine star because he's not reacting with proper pathos to the fact his human pal has just been gunned down. The trainer, desperate to appeal to the dog's sense of method acting, pleads with him to recall his most painful moment. The scene dissolves to the dog's blissful memory of trying to catch a passing Budweiser truck by leaping the fence — and crashing his nose right into it. Back on the set, he is now howling with such convincing agony that the entire crew is weeping.

What may look like an amusing sketch concocted to sell beer only works — even from an advertising standpoint — because it has all the elements necessary to communicate a complete plot:

> The Cast: The dog and the Hollywood crew.
> The Locations: The Western set and the dog's front yard.
> The Problem (BEGINNING): The dog will lose his job if he can't project sadness.
> The Attempt to Resolve (MIDDLE): Flashback/memory sequence.
> The Resolution (END): By recalling his most painful moment, the dog summons the necessary emotion to make the scene a howling success.

On a final note, keep in mind that commercial advertising is all designed to sell us on one of four concepts: food, sex, self-esteem, and security. With the exception of food (not counting popcorn, of course), movies — regardless of their length — are out to sell us on the very same things. The shorter the playing time, the more obvious your "product's" relationship and significance to the audience needs to be.

CINEMA CHALLENGE

Write your screenplay idea as a 60-second short, applying what you have just learned about commercials.

RECOMMENDED WEB SITE

Every year, the advertising industry bestows prestigious worldwide awards called "Clios" for excellence in TV, Radio, Print, Design, Internet, Outdoor, and Integrated Media. In addition to Clio festivals, screenings of the award-winning ads are shown throughout major cities, as well as compiled in collector editions sold directly through their Web site at *www.clioawards.com*. The entertainment value of seeing the best of the best is as noteworthy as the tips and tricks you'll glean for making your own films click from start to finish.

IDEA-STARTERS

Commercials provide a ready source of scenarios from which to develop ideas for shorts.

> › Pick any commercial that is either currently airing or one from the past that was memorable enough to have stuck with you.
> › Assign names to the characters (if they don't already have them).
> › Decide what their central issue is going to be.
> › Using the commercial as the beginning of your story, develop a 10-minute script with a middle and an ending.

> EXAMPLE: Remember the General Foods International Coffee® commercial in which two women friends are fondly reminiscing about their trip to Europe and, in particular, a certain Frenchman who set their pulses aflutter? What would happen if he were to stroll into their lives again at that very moment? Will his handsome looks now trigger fierce competition and jealousy? Or with the passage of years, did this same monsieur consume a tad more Brie and pastry than he really should have?

TALL ORDERS FOR SHORT STUFF

For aspiring screenwriters, the ability to create memorable shorts serves a two-fold purpose:

The first is to provide a home for those plots that simply aren't meaty enough to fill up a screen for two hours. Because they generally take less time to write and less money to produce than features, they also constitute a faster track to building a diversified screen portfolio. The second is to fill the needs of a growing market of indie and student filmmakers seeking scripts that can be used in film festivals and competitions as demonstration of their directorial and production skills. While the pay is usually low and/or on a deferred comp basis, you'll still get a credit and a copy of the finished product.

Nor should you ignore the fact that shorts ranging from two to 30 minutes and developed specifically for Internet viewing have become "virtual resumes" for prospective producers to scope out writing, acting, and directing talent for future projects. As access becomes more and more of a two-way street, the demand for original material will translate into showcase opportunities for newcomers that were previously limited.

The insular nature of shorts as a medium allows screenwriters to explore and concentrate on one facet of a character's life rather than execute a major personality makeover. To return to the earlier-referenced Budweiser commercial, the only issue that concerns us in this 60-second tableau is whether the dog will be able to perform convincingly. Whether he has litter-mate rivalries, abandonment issues with his mother, distrust of his trainer, or feels that he deserves a bigger dressing room never comes up. Nor does it invite any speculation of where his tail-wagging career might go next. We as the audience know that he's going to do fine, given the positive outcome of this brief slice of life we have just been privy to.

Where feature films strive to make life bigger than it actually is, shorts tend to mirror life from a workaday perspective and, thereby, involve the audience on more of an interpersonal level. They originate from those experiences which strike a universal chord and, unlike a studio feature that endeavors to wrap up all loose ends, a successful short can plant seeds of introspection which will continue to grow after the final roll of credits.

Keep this simplistic layout in mind as you go through the process of deciding which of your ideas might make for compelling shorts. The objective here isn't to see how well you can scrunch a big plot into a tiny box, but rather how you can isolate a select *dimension* of that big plot and allow audiences to experience its emotional depth at a level they would have missed in the context of a longer story.

The following movie excerpt demonstrates how this principle works in defining your own story's external boundaries and internal focus.

In *Robin Hood, Prince of Thieves* (1991), there is a melodramatic (some might even say sappy) moment when Kevin Costner tearfully grabs Christian Slater and acknowledges him as his heretofore unmentioned younger brother, Will Scarlet. Although Robin subsequently saves his life at Nottingham and even invites him to dress up and come to the wedding, there are never any "bro bonding" scenes in which these two lads sit down, throw back a couple of Friar Tuck's beers, and discuss their innermost feelings.

Why not? Well, aside from the fact that moviegoers really wouldn't care at this point, such a scene would impede the more necessary task of rescuing Maid Marian before she can become Mrs. Sheriff.

Suppose, however, that the theme of sibling reconciliation appeals to you as a development project. Because the intent of your short is to zero in on the newly discovered relationship between these half-brothers, everything else depicted in the film would be extraneous. The here-and-now window through which we view Robin and Will's interaction doesn't require that we resolve all of the issues of the past (i.e., "Did Dad really like you best?") nor address any contingencies of the future (i.e., "Can I come and live with you and Marian?").

As one of my clients succinctly put it, "A short simply *is*."

USING ONE-ACT PLAYS AS A STARTING POINT

Back when I first began testing the commercial waters with my plays, I was dismayed to discover that producers and publishers were only interested in reading full-length scripts. One-acts, the likes of which I was penning for my acting company, simply weren't considered a viable venue at the time.

Although a trio or quartet of short works united by a common theme certainly offer a more equitable distribution of roles for school and community actors, it wasn't until fairly recently that the theatrical equivalent of a short really caught on as a program alternative. Today, many competitions not only offer a one-act division, but distill the category even further to include entries of 10 minutes duration.

It is in this particular category that you can easily test whether your movie idea is structurally suited to a short-film format. Unlike two and three act works which are sometimes too talky and physically static to adapt to a feature, short plays lend themselves extremely well. After all, they already contain the minimalist elements of cast, setting, and scope inherent in this screenwriting genre, freeing the author to switch over and substitute the eye of the camera for the collective eye of the audience.

One-act plays for study can readily be found in published anthologies at your local library or bookstore or through magazine and catalogue subscription services such as Plays, Inc., Meriwether Publishing, and Eldridge Publishing. In addition, theater-related newsletters such as *Insight for Playwrights* (*www.writersinsight.com*) provide monthly contest information for festivals, regional production, and publication.

IDEA-STARTERS

Each of the following set-ups would lend itself to a 20-minute short. Select the one you like best and identify:

1. The emotional tone you'd like to communicate;
2. The characters;
3. The setting(s);
4. The outcome (which can be positive *or* negative); and
5. The experience(s) you can draw from your own background that would enable you to write a credible script.

> A housewife arrives home from the store and realizes she has accidentally shoplifted a tube of lipstick.
> A young man receives the news that a girl he was cruel to at the previous night's dance has committed suicide.
> A real estate agent mistakenly assumes that the burglar she has encountered is a prospective buyer for the house she is showing.
> A businessman discovers that a neighborhood panhandler is someone he once envied in high school.
> Sibling allegiance is put to the test when one of them needs a kidney from the other.

SECTION

3

WORKING IT OUT

CHAPTER 11 | THE REALITIES OF REVISION

Four years ago, a friend of mine started writing her first screenplay. She's still writing it. She also has yet to complete the first scene. It's not that she's lacking in inspiration or free time, however. It's that she's spending all of her energy on rewrites that no one has even requested.

Obviously, she's not alone in the mindset that every word and thought has to be perfect before it can be sent out. While it goes without saying that presentation, spelling, and punctuation always should adhere to that rule, writers do themselves a huge disservice by trying to second-guess what someone else is going to want changed. Time and again, I've labored over eloquent narratives, only to have an editor "X" out the entire passage. On the flip side, I've penned throwaway lines just to put down *some*thing and received back-slapping "Bravos." Go figure.

Bottom line: Always write your first draft from the heart and show it to someone whose opinion counts before you even *start* the deconstruction process.

WHAT DO YOU MEAN IT NEEDS 'FIXING'?

The year after I graduated from high school, my very first play — a western melodrama entitled *West* — was produced. I share the following anecdote as a dose of reality for starry-eyed screenwriters who believe that everything they have put into their scripts will translate, line for line, to the finished product. It doesn't.

My initial euphoria as the lights went down in the theater quickly segued to one big "Arghgh" as the curtains parted and the first two actors walked out on stage. "How could they have gotten the town setting so blatantly wrong?" I thought. "And who are these two actors supposed to be playing?" Certainly they couldn't be the sheriff and his long-suffering deputy, two personas who were so meticulously described in the cast list.

The moment they opened their mouths, even further discrepancies revealed themselves. A part of me wanted to jump out of my seat and start explaining to the audience that this wasn't the way I had written it at all. Another part of me wanted to just slump further into the cushions and pray that no one dared introduce me as the author at the end of it.

During intermission, I sought out the director and, in as calm a voice as I could muster, remarked that the play looked a smidge different from what I remembered writing.

"Oh that," she nonchalantly replied. "I always wanted to try my hand at fixing a script. I didn't think you'd mind..."

Such is the fate awaiting you once you've typed FADE OUT and sent your creation out into the world to be discovered. On the one hand, you can't wait for someone to fall in love with it and want to produce it. On the other hand, a part of you is dreading how much they're going to screw it up and turn it into something you no longer even recognize.

Depending on the terms of your option agreement with a producer, you may or may not be brought in to do the rewrites for it. While extra work usually doesn't equate to any extra money — especially with smaller studios — neither does it mean that any money or recognition will be taken away from you if a second or third screenwriter takes the helm. Whatever happens from this point forward has still flowed forth from your original concept, a condition which, accordingly, still will be acknowledged when they roll the credits.

Obviously, if the rewrite responsibilities are taken out of your control, there's really nothing you can do about it. Instead of venting or vexing, take that energy and go apply it to your next script.

Easier said than done, yes.

Having brought this baby into the world, you might like nothing better than to hold its hand for as long as possible. Suffice it to say, however, this insular approach cuts off the chance of it being groomed by others who are perhaps more worldly and better traveled in this journey called filmmaking.

On the flip-side, you *may* be asked to participate, incorporating those changes that the power-brokers think would make for a better movie. How you respond to that invitation (or directive, as it were) depends on the following perceptions of what the rewrite process means to you on a personal level.

GROUSING ALL THE WAY

We all have a possessive streak when it comes to our own work. Woe to the critic who dares to suggest we've got a comma out of place or that we used an incorrect word. Or what of the reader who shows undisguised ignorance of Marjorie's motivation to get back together with Chad or completely overlooks what you thought was a darned clever allegory to the curse of Jonah?

Good grief! Are these people stupid or what?

While you certainly can content yourself with the secret opinion that, yes, they *do* have the functional IQ of paste, it wouldn't do to voice that out loud to those who hold the key to your cinematic future. Nor would it behoove you to say "yes" if it's with the intention of protesting throughout the entire exercise.

A hard lesson for writers of any medium to accept is that editors, agents, and producers really aren't out to make you look like a rube. They want the project to be just as successful as you want it to be. As such, the changes they recommend are to maximize the story's good points, minimize or eliminate its flaws, and to flesh out those areas that aren't as well developed as they should be.

CHOOSING YOUR BATTLES

Provided you don't turn obsessive about it, you can sometimes negotiate compromise on a script revision. If there is something that you really feel needs to stay in for the sake of integrity, you can certainly broach the subject with the producer. That said, of course, you need to be amenable when he/she comes back and says "no" on something else.

If you *are* going to go to battle for a particular issue, make sure that you can back it up with a more substantive argument than "just because."

In my Scottish time travel, *The Spellbox*, there is a magnificent deerhound named Citi. One of my trademarks, in fact, is to always write dogs into my various plots and assign them names of actual dogs I have known and loved. Furthermore, nothing terrible ever happens to any of the beasts in my books or scripts, a welcome change, I think, from authors who introduce gratuitous violence against animals, children, and women just to get a rise out of the audience.

When I went into negotiations with the film's producers, I made it clear that not only was the dog to be spared any harm during potential rewrites but that they couldn't change her name, either. To my delight, I learned that both partners were dog lovers just like myself. "In other words," they said, "all the humans in this are expendable, but the dog—"

"Right," I replied. "The dog stays in the picture."

I like to think that, somewhere over the Rainbow Bridge, the real Citi is wagging her tail at having her own clause in a film contract.

SOMETHING TO BE LEARNED

Some of the best screenwriting training you can get is of the hands-on variety. When someone asks you to do rewrites, think of it as a living classroom in which to hone your craft. It's also a stellar chance to demonstrate how cooperative and flexible you are, a bonus when it comes to future script submissions and/or assignments on collaborative projects with other professionals.

Between the structured direction (i.e., "Shorten Lucy's speech at the top of page 19") and the collective brainstorming (i.e., "Here are some location ideas we've been tossing around for the kidnapping scene"), you'll be picking up invaluable tips on how to look at your script through a different set of eyes.

And remember this: whatever characters, lines, jokes, or nuances end up on the cutting room floor can always be swept up and resurrected to fit your *next* script.

THE CARE AND FEEDING OF CRITIQUE GROUPS

Are there fellow screenwriters in your community who get together on a regular basis to share their work? If there are, find out how to join them. If there aren't, there's no reason you couldn't start a group yourself. Getting together with like-minded individuals not only keeps you encouraged and on track with deadlines, but provides a built-in cast to read each other's scenes out loud.

Depending on the work habits and availability of your peers, your meetings probably will be scheduled once a month or once every two months. It's also important that you keep the size of your critique group fairly small to allow equal participation in readings and discussions. When I mentored a women's writing group in Northern California, the membership was limited to six, rotating at each writer's house for either a potluck, a weekend breakfast, or an evening of wine and cheese, while we read each other's new works.

The only cautionary note you may want to take heed of is not to let everyone else in the group rewrite your script to the point you no longer recognize it. Because they are writers themselves, there will be a natural tendency for them — and you — to want to rip out the seams, break out the dye, shorten the hem, embroider the sleeves, add a ruffle, and replace all the buttons on a creation that the author believed looked pretty nice to begin with. Accept any criticism with a grain of salt, incorporating those that you feel comfortable with and ignoring those that aren't a good fit.

Most of all, be supportive of each other... and have fun!

CHAMPAGNE TASTES AND HAMBURGER BUDGETS

Sometimes the only thing standing between your script and a sale is a price tag. My work as a coverage consultant can attest to the disconnect that exists between having something creative to say and believing that a gazillionaire's budget is the only way to achieve it. While technological wizardry has enabled Hollywood to craft mystical creatures and entire realms from cyber scratch (Al Pacino's film, *Simone*, even extends this cinemagic to the creation of a human "star"), a lot of script readers won't commit themselves past the first page if a novice has peppered it with gratuitous "grandness" and expenses that exceed what's on the projected ledger.

One of my clients, for instance, was penning a Western epic that included a scene in which 80 Indian braves are seated outside a cluster of teepees as their squaws cook a bunch of elk over campfires. The scene, which lasted only 20 seconds, contained three lines of dialogue, one of which was a throwaway comment about when dinner would be ready.

"Why do you need 80 braves in non-speaking parts?" I queried.

"I thought they'd make a nice backdrop," he said.

Suffice it to say, a producer with a modest budget won't be enamored with paying scale to 80 actors plus procuring costumes, makeup, wigs, teepees, and a couple hefty elk just to be nice window-dressing, especially when those three lines could be dropped completely for not advancing the plot or being conveyed in a tight shot against a backdrop of trees.

The fact that none of these 80 Indians would ever be seen again in the storyline, nor recycled to play other parts, was an additional liability. The script was further hindered by death-defying canoe rides down the rapids, a stampede of wild horses, and the recreation of historic towns which long ago fell by the American wayside.

If "location, location, location" is the buzzword of real estate, "budget, budget, budget" is what governs moviemaking.

Back when I ran a touring theater company, there was only one rule regarding the amount of furniture and props written into a show: If It Doesn't Fit in the Car, It's Not Going. It was this sense of economy that most influenced what I carried over into my workshops for aspiring scriptwriters, reinforcing the philosophy that if no one is going to mention why there's a moosehead above the mantle, maybe that moosehead really doesn't need to be there. A good story, first and foremost, needs to succeed on the strength of its plot and characters, not the weightiness of its production budget.

Movies on the cheap. Bowfinger, *starring Steve Martin and Eddie Murphy, is not only a tongue-in-cheek send-up of the film industry but a humorous primer on how* not *to get a picture made.* (Bowfinger, *Imagine Entertainment/Universal, 1999.*)

While everyone hungers to write a cast-of-thousands epic with a wealth of complex sets and technical glitz, the reality is that the lower the author can keep a script's costs, the higher the chances of a sale.

What kind of red flags does your own movie idea contain?

The following quiz can help you identify them before you ever start shopping your script to a producer.

1. My film is (A) Contemporary; (B) Contemporary with historical flashbacks; or (C) Historical or Futuristic.

2. My film has (A) 0-10 special effects; (B) 11-30 special effects; or (C) over 30 special effects.

3. My film has (A) less than 10 actors; (B) 11-50 actors; or (C) over 50 actors.

4. My film has (A) no animals in it; (B) animals that are strictly for atmosphere (i.e., grazing cows, sleeping cats, etc.) or (C) animals that have a defined role or do special tricks.

5. My film has (A) 0-10 interior scenes; (B) 11-30 interior scenes; or (C) over 30 interior scenes. (Note: If you have three scenes that take place in the same location [for instance, a kitchen], count them as only one interior no matter how many times it is used.)

6. My film has (A) 0-10 exterior scenes; (B) 11-30 exterior scenes; or (C) over 30 exterior scenes. (Note: If you have three scenes that take place in the same location [such as a park], count them as only 1 exterior. If, however, you have a scene in a park, a scene at a beach, and a scene at an outdoor café, that would be 3 exteriors.)

7. My film has (A) fewer than 10 night scenes; (B) 11-20 night scenes; or (C) over 20 night scenes. (Note: Night scenes are those which take place outdoors and in the dark, not just evening scenes which are all shot inside a house.)

8. My film has (A) no car scenes or simply street scenes where cars are part of the background; (B) scenes in which my characters are traveling by car; or (C) car chases, crashes, or explosions.

9. My film primarily takes place (A) on a soundstage; (B) in an existing house or public structure; or (C) in a specially constructed set (i.e., a 'Medieval' castle built from scratch for the production).

10. My film would be most successful with (A) a cast of unknowns; (B) one name star; (C) three or more name stars.

1 1. Physical stunts in my film are (A) non-existent; (B) computer-generated; or (C) performed by stunt people.

12. For scenes outside a soundstage, the majority of my film takes place (A) in a small town; (B) in a major American city; or (c) in a foreign country.

To score: For each (A) answer, give yourself 1 point. For each (B) answer, give yourself 5 points. For each (C) answer, give yourself 10 points.

Before we take a look at what your total score means, here are some points to keep in mind that impact the overall cost of a screenplay.

1. Contemporary plots are usually less costly than period pieces. Can the story you want to tell be told in a modern context or are the historical benchmarks central to your characters' viewpoints and actions? For futuristic tableaus, how do you intend to craft ahead-of-the-times architecture, vehicles, planets, etc.?

2. Fires, floods, earthquakes, volcanoes, explosions — while many disasters can now be computer-generated, those that can't are going to cost money and plenty of it.

3. Do you really need those swarming crowds? Even though they're paid scale for just taking up space, they're still an expense. (And probably whatever they've got hanging at home in their closets won't match your creative vision.)

4. Anything with animals — especially trained ones — could be a big-ticket item. Not to mention the presence of the SPCA on the set to ensure humane treatment and safety for anything that swims, flies, or moves on four feet.

5. Exterior scenes leave the crew at the mercy of time, season, and weather, as opposed to interior shots which will look exactly the same whether it's 3 a.m. in the dead of winter or 7:30 on a summer night.

6. Night scenes are more expensive to film than scenes in daylight.

7. Are your car chases/crashes necessary or just gratuitous? Vehicular mayhem can put a sizable dent in the budget.

8. Going on location is pricier than shooting on a soundstage, especially the travel factor. It may be cheaper to shoot in a foreign country, but in exchange for their cooperation and city hospitality, you'll probably be expected to stay in their hotels, frequent their restaurants, and — oh yes — fill out the cast and crew with star-struck locals.

9. Specifying that "Mel Gibson has to be in this movie or it simply won't work" probably isn't a compelling pitch.

10. Every time the equipment gets moved, the cash register dings. Try to minimize your locations so multiple scenes can be shot in one place. It's also prudent to take into account the expense of a scene versus the amount of time it's actually seen on camera, i.e., remember those 80 Indians?

How did your answers tally up?

If your score is less than 40, you probably have a story that falls into the "low" budget range and would be appealing to a small or independent producer.

If your score is between 40 and 80, you have hit the mid-range. This range gives you a lot of latitude since you can adjust up or down, depending on whom you approach with your pitch.

If your score is between 80 and 120, your vision may be too "big budget" for someone to take a risk on. The good news? It's within your power to bring the higher numbers down by examining your (C) answers and determining where appropriate compromises can be made without compromising the story.

CHAPTER 12 | MAKING THE MOST OF
PROFESSIONAL CONSULTATION

One of the terms you'll often encounter on the path to being a screenwriter is "script coverage." Script coverage actually refers to two different levels of critique. The first type is done by studio readers whose job is to give each project either a pass (thumbs down) or a recommend (thumbs up). What they are looking for — and subsequently summarizing in one page or less — are projects that are not only professionally packaged but are in keeping with the studio's corporate vision, budget, and wish list.

You, as the writer, won't be privy to what appears in a studio critique unless you have someone inside the system who can find out for you. Therefore, should your submission receive a polite "No, thanks," you'll have no clue whether they thought your premise of flesh-eating hamsters from Saturn was a singularly stupid idea or if it had too many similarities to a flick on flesh-eating woodchucks from Akron they had already optioned three months earlier.

While rejection without explanation is one of the more frustrating realities of this business, the sheer volume of material received and the shortage of personnel to process all of it makes it impossible to counsel individual writers on why their work didn't click.

The second type of coverage is a paid critique that screenwriters *do* see. Unlike the pass/recommend format, this type is designed to address the strengths and weaknesses of a project in the context of a teaching tool for the writer to improve his/her craft. Coverage consultants (who may or may not be affiliated with a studio or agency) are either generalists or specialize in specific genres (i.e., romantic comedies) or aspects of screenwriting (i.e., character development).

The fees charged for coverage services vary in accordance with expertise, level of detail and recommendation provided, and whether the client wants to engage in an ongoing mentor relationship. While script consultants are fairly easy to find on the Internet and in the classified sections of screen trade magazines, finding one who is committed to giving you honest and practical advice is a little harder. Just as there are unscrupulous therapists who prolong the recovery of patients who represent a long-term meal-ticket, there are also all manner of "script doctors" whose method of cure has more to do with reducing your bank account than maximizing your talent.

Certainly one of the best ways to find professional assistance is through word of mouth. If you know of fellow screenwriters who have engaged the services of a script consultant and were pleased with the feedback they received, find out whether you can be referred to them. Screenwriter chat rooms are also a good place to post your query and garner a wide variety of suggestions... including which ones to stay away from.

If you haven't already bookmarked the following Web sites, you'll find them to be a good source of consultants who are not only accomplished writers themselves but who additionally have worked as agents, entertainment lawyers, directors, and producers.

> American Screenwriters Association
  www.asascreenwriters.com
> InkTip
  www.inktip.com
> Writers Guild of America
  www.wga.org
> MovieBytes
  www.moviebytes.com/directory.cfm
  (Note: This directory lists contests that are sponsored by coverage consultants, as well as studio competitions that provide feedback to each entrant.)

Did you hear a good speaker at your last screenwriters' conference? There is a strong network of writing professionals who are always more than happy to make referrals to colleagues and/or recommend courses in which one-on-one feedback is a major component. If you subscribe to trade magazines such as *Screentalk*, *MovieMaker Magazine* and *Scr(i)pt*, you may want to extend your sleuthing to the bios of contributing authors and editors, many of whom do independent consulting and referrals.

What can you expect to get back in terms of professional advice? Again, this is contingent upon the background of the consultants and the value of their time. For my own clients, I provide five to eight single-spaced pages of analysis covering the following areas: originality, character development, dialogue, pacing, structure, budget, and marketability. In addition — and dependent on a submission's degree of polish — I recommend upcoming competitions, Web sites, and independent studios that I feel would make a good match.

While this type of consultation works well for many writers in identifying what kind of first-aid their scripts need, others will seek out someone who can do a line-by-line analysis of the full text and, if necessary, participate in an actual rewrite. For those who are just starting out, consultants who can provide mini-critiques of the first 10-20 pages, plus a synopsis, are all they really need to let them know if they're on the right track.

Keep in mind, of course, the subjective nature of this exercise. One of the caveats I always include in my own coverage notes is that it is up to the individual writer whether or not to incorporate the recommendations into subsequent drafts. Certainly the more people you invite to read your work, the better handle you have on how it's going to be received by a broader audience. Just because you have paid someone money to render a critique of your work doesn't mean that his or her opinion is more valuable than nine friends of yours from college who just read it for free. What it does mean, however, is that you are tapping the expertise of an industry pro who can provide solid guidance on how to fix trouble spots that may be keeping your work from getting produced.

That said, you need to remember why you engaged the consultant's services to begin with, especially if the critique you receive is less glowing than what you were anticipating. For as many clients as I mentor who come away with a clearer understanding of what needs to be done to make their work stand up to scrutiny and tough competition, I have an equal number who take a defensive stance and spend more time arguing than learning.

The following story illustrates this point.

Several years ago, I was approached by an earnest middle manager named Wally who was obsessed with the Lewis and Clark Expedition and wanted my professional advice in penning an epic film about it. While the source of Wally's particular fixation was never really made clear during the entire time he was a client, I nonetheless felt compelled to point out to him that (1) it had already been done and (2) Lewis and Clark don't exactly spring to the forefront as riveting, cinematic giants.

Wally, however, was insistent on pursuing his vision. After all, he explained, the expedition's 200th anniversary was approaching and he was confident that he was the only one who had been paying any attention to the calendar.

> NOTE TO EPIC FEATURE WRITERS | Studios that film historical adventures tend to keep track of these things and start planning for them 5-10 years in advance. If the event holds enough commercial substance, you can bet someone else already has it in the queue.

The most challenging aspect of such films, of course, is that historical events themselves are either the end-game or accidental by-product of a much larger succession of celestial happenings. From the standpoint of a contemporary audience, the farther removed they perceive themselves to be from "So how does any of this 'old news' affect me personally?" the harder it is to convince the powers-that-be to fund it. Relevance to 21st century viewers has to clearly outvote whatever relevance the event itself had to the people who experienced it first-hand.

Historical retrospectives also are hard to manage from a structural level. Starting the plot from the very first domino that set the rest in motion can make for a story that's too long. On the flip side, starting the action at the denouement can result in a tale which then has nowhere to go except into recap and reminiscence.

The additional encumbrance of an audience already knowing what the denouement *is* (i.e., the North wins, the ship sinks, the president gets assassinated) necessitates the author having to explore the existing body of knowledge through an alternative dimension and/or viewpoint. The question of *what* is going to happen accordingly assumes less importance than *how* and *why* it will impact the various characters involved. More often than not, the crisis represents a platform for social commentary, affirming that only under the most extenuating state of affairs will the best and worst of human nature be revealed.

> RULE NO. 1 | If it takes too much exposition to establish what the core conflict is going to be, it won't work as a feature film. Audiences don't have the patience to watch "reel" life played out and chronologically explained in "real" time.

Not only did Wally's initial draft ignore the excessive backstory rules of screenwriting but he chose to make as his lead character a fictional lieutenant through which the wild and woolly adventures in the Pacific Northwest would be experienced. (Sort of a Greek chorus, if you will, on why Thomas Jefferson was so keen on the westward expansion plan to begin with.)

He began the script with the young lieutenant's stint at West Point and from there segued to a nostalgic visit home to his invalid mother, his strict and unloving alcoholic father, and his younger sister who was engaged to his best friend's brother who had originally contemplated the priesthood but changed his mind when—

Whoa! Wasn't this supposed to be an epic about Meriwether Lewis and William Clark? What are all these other people doing here?

Wally maintained that the lieutenant's dysfunctional family life was critical to the plot, especially since said lieutenant was going to meet an equally fictitious Indian princess along the way and that Sacagawea would be instrumental in convincing the princess' father not to bash the lieutenant's brains out on the nearest rock.

Hmmm. This was beginning to sound like *Pocahontas* meets *Dances With Wolves*.

I recommended to him that if his intention was to glorify the accomplishments and heroics of the people on the expedition, he'd be better served to stick with those who were actually *on* it. Considering that this was probably one of the most thoroughly documented travels of its time, thrusting at least two fictional characters into its finite midst — 39 humans and 1 dog — would be sure to incur the wrath of the very history buffs whom Wally was trying to court as his primary audience.

In fairness, of course, even the 1955 version of this intrepid excursion into the wilderness was marred by the inclusion of Barbara Hale as a separate love interest for the two feuding frontiersmen (Fred MacMurray and Charlton Heston) in order to deflect potential controversy over an interracial romance involving Sacagawea.

That the latter was winsomely played by Donna Reed, of course, was supposed to be overlooked. Suffice it to say, 1950s moviegoers were more likely to forgive a multitude of creative-license sins than 21st century critics who thrive on exposing mistakes and posting them on the Internet.

With historically based plots that utilize gladiators, refugees, soldiers, peasant uprisings, shipwrecks, or anything else involving hordes of humanity, there's no problem fabricating a few personas. It's only when you try to add an extra astronaut or slip an additional wife into Henry the Eighth's bed that you're courting cinematic disaster.

RULE NO. 2 | If the personalities of the key players in the history-making event can't sustain a two-hour story on their own, it is either (1) a weak plot that should be abandoned or (2) the event itself needs to recede into the background of one of its secondary participants or a fictionalized character who could credibly have been present.

Since my client was determined to see this epic through to completion, I instructed him to draw up a list of those members of the expedition whose real lives would best lend themselves to a feature screenplay. In addition to the obvious trio of Lewis, Clark, and Sacagawea, he added Charbonneau (Sacagawea's common-law husband), Jean Baptiste (their infant son) and York, Clark's African American manservant to whom Clark repeatedly denied freedom until 1811. (My own contribution to the list was Seaman, Lewis' black Newfoundland, who accompanied the party.)

Why make up phony lieutenants and Indian princesses, I reiterated, when he already had such a rich cast to draw from? Even the lesser known privates, boatmen and scouts — several of whom later went on to have wilderness adventures of their own — could provide a compelling perspective on what transpired during the long journey westward.

It was Sacagawea whom Wally finally deemed was not only the most enigmatic of the team, but the one whose unhappy personal life was mostly likely to resonate with modern viewers, especially females. Here, after all, was a woman who is one of history's two most famous Native American heroines and yet no one can say with any certainty what exactly happened to her after the group's return to St. Louis.

One faction claims that she died shortly after the expedition's conclusion. Since Charbonneau by then had acquired several Indian "wives," the death of any one of them could easily have been misconstrued and publicized as that of "Bird Woman," the same young girl who accompanied the Corps of Discovery. Another faction, however — specifically, her own tribe — relates that she eventually returned to them, lived well into her 90s, and was buried wearing the Jefferson medallion around her neck which had been presented by no less than the president himself.

While we do know for a fact that William Clark assumed the role of her young son's legal guardian at her own request and was responsible for his schooling in Europe, this raises even more questions.

> What would compel a devoted mother to give up that which was the most precious thing in the world to her?
> Did she know that she was dying and wanted to ensure that her son would be well taken care of?
> Was Charbonneau an abusive or distant father from whom she wanted to protect Jean Baptiste?
> Was there an unrequited attraction between Sacagawea and Clark, complicated not only by the difference in ethnicity, but by their respective marriages to other people?
> Was Jean Baptiste an unwelcome reminder of her association with Charbonneau whom she could easily live without?
> Did she believe that her mixed-breed son would ultimately fare better in the white man's environment than he would if she took him back to live among her own people?
> Who's really buried in Sacagawea's grave? What if she related her adventures to another of Charbonneau's female companions prior to her death, even going so far as to give away the Jefferson

medallion as a gift? Pre-dating the Anna Anderson/Anastasia charade, could the woman who lived out her years as the well-traveled Sacagawea have been, in fact, a pretender?

Reinvigorated by all of this mystique about the expedition's only female, Wally embarked on his second draft.

```
EXT. - TEEPEES - DAY
There is much rejoicing in the tribe as they welcome
the birth of a new baby girl.
```

> RULE NO. 3 | People are not born interesting. They only become interesting through age and experience. Don't start your story at the beginning of their lives. Start it at the beginning of when their lives take on significant meaning to the rest of us.

By page 85 of Wally's new and supposedly improved version, Sacagawea had yet to even meet her French trapper husband, much less encounter the two white explorers with whom her name would become inextricably linked throughout history.

"When, exactly, are you going to get to the expedition part?" I asked.

Unlike a novel where an author has the luxury of cradle-to-grave minutia, a screenplay demands that one's lifespan either be sped up to the equivalent of dog-years (i.e., *Braveheart* or *Amadeus*) or focus on those traits or incidents which are directly illustrative of the character's sense of self or purpose (i.e., *Wilde* or *Jefferson in Paris*).

While Sacagawea's kidnapping as a child and subsequent enslavement by a rival tribe until her teens certainly had bearing on her world outlook, these don't have to be spelled out in linear fashion in order for us to know who she is in 1804. For that matter, even her presence *during* the course of the journey isn't going to hold our attention unless it promises to reveal something which we hadn't already gleaned from elementary school history books.

> RULE NO. 4 | **Make every word of dialogue count.**

What should have been Wally's third-time's-the-charm attempt at recreating early 19th century history was still falling flat. Although he was now utilizing a bookend approach whereby Clark and Sacagawea are reunited a year after the expedition, their initial dialogue consisted mostly of "So how have you been? Fine, thanks, and you? Well, I've been pretty busy lately re-reading my journals. Would you like to see them? Oh yes, that would be nice..."

"Cut the chit-chat," I advised Wally. "Open the film on a dark and stormy night in St. Louis." A cloaked figure carrying a large bundle is anxiously searching the houses for a particular address. She finds it and knocks on the door. A moment later, Clark's housekeeper informs him that he has a visitor, a "savage" woman who claims to know him. When he learns that this midnight caller is none other than Sacagawea, accompanied by her toddler son, he immediately invites her in.

With nary a word yet spoken between them, our curiosity is already aroused regarding their relationship.

> Why is she out on such a stormy night?
> Where is Charbonneau?
> Where is Clark's wife?
> Why has she brought her child with her?
> What were the circumstances under which they last parted?
> What does she want from him now?

My client was enthused about this and excitedly continued the scenario with Clark sending his housekeeper next door to borrow some warm clothes from the neighbors.

Oddly — or perhaps just because Wally is a guy — the only loaner ensemble available was the latest, low-cut Parisian fashion and the requisite jewelry and hair combs. When Clark next sees her in the doorway of his study, Sacagawea has miraculously transformed into — "Catherine Zeta Jones would be good," Wally opined. "What do you think?"

What I think is that I'm not paid nearly enough to read this stuff.

> RULE NO. 5 | Deliver what you promise and stay on message. If you start meandering, your audience will be led astray as well and get annoyed with you.

In Wally's Catherine Zeta Jones opening, the implication can be drawn that this film will be a romance. "And maybe," Wally optimistically envisioned, "her husband Michael could be talked into playing Clark..."

All right. We can go with the romance angle. Except that the first flashback after he tells her how beautiful she is makes a sudden splash into raging rapids, marauding bears, blood, gore, and dissension among the men about whether Jefferson is just sending them all on a wild goose chase to further his own ambitions.

Action.
Adventure.
Hot-headed politics.
Breathtaking scenery.
Native American mysticism.
Rivalry and fisticuffs.

Those sensuous, meaningful glances earlier exchanged in the doorway between Bird-Woman and the besotted William are now entirely forgotten as the Corps of Discovery grumbles its way westward and encounters hostile Indians, bad weather, poisonous snakes, and occasional documentary-style voice overs regarding their progress.

It's one thing to keep an audience guessing where you're going next. Flat-out confusing them by genre-switching is taboo. While history itself doesn't neatly color within the lines, you — as the writer — are still obligated to do so. If your idea can't be compartmentalized into a recognizable category that you can sustain for 90+ pages, you're going to be scattered too far over the map to execute a cohesive story.

> RULE NO. 6 | Sometimes there's a good reason why you can't/shouldn't/better not go home again.

I reminded Wally once again about the existence of *The Far Horizons*, the MacMurray/Heston film made back in 1955 and eventually reissued in video under the title *The Untamed West*. In 1997, Ken Burns literally retraced the footsteps of the famous expedition in a documentary narrated by Hal Holbrook. Other than that....

Wally interpreted the four-decade gap as the requisite validation that movie audiences were due for a reintroduction. I diplomatically proposed a different explanation: maybe this particular chapter of American history doesn't really excite anyone. Unlike Wyatt Earp, George Armstrong Custer, Jesse James, Billy the Kid, Wild Bill Hickock, and Buffalo Bill Cody whose personas have been centerstage in 26-54 movies and scores more of cameos and documentaries, Lewis and Clark's "star-power" sadly didn't extend much beyond their return to Missouri.

That's not to say they weren't men of courage and historical merit. It just says that you don't want to embark on a script that will keep begging the question, "Are we there yet?"

At the end of almost five months, Wally announced that he was terminating our relationship because he felt I didn't like his script as much as he thought I should. "I'm going to find someone who's more supportive," he said.

The best I could hope, of course, was that he'd find someone who'd tell him pretty much the same things I did. Unfortunately — and to paraphrase P.T. Barnum — there will be two to take him, charge him much more and tell him that he's brilliant. The film will never get made... and, sadly, the Wally's of the world will never understand why.

SCREENWRITER'S CHECKLIST

If you decide to get a professional evaluation of your work, the following things should be taken into consideration.

> What are your expectations of the critique? (i.e., an evaluation of your strengths and weaknesses, a referral to a studio or agent, a mentoring relationship).

> What are the qualifications of the consultant who will be reviewing your script? What do others have to say about the quality of their work?

> What can you afford to spend on script coverage? Since fees range from less than $100 to over $1,000, it pays to shop around.

> What kind of timeframe is involved between submission and receipt of a coverage document? (Note: If you're planning to enter the script into competition, allow at least 4-6 weeks in order to have the coverage done and address the recommended changes.)

> Do you need the entire script reviewed or just a few scenes that you feel are cumbersome? Some consultants, such as myself, will do mini-appraisals that not only save you money but enable you to assess whether you could have a comfortable relationship.

> How well do you feel you handle criticism?
> Are there provisions in place for follow-up questions with the consultant after receipt of his/her critique of your script?
> Is the consultant amenable to second-reads of the same material at either a reduced fee or gratis?

AUTHOR, KNOW THY SCRIPT

Before you engage a professional consultant to analyze your work, there are some standard questions that you will probably be asked. The form I developed for my own clients is one that not only clues me in on the storyline and the author's background but has application to his/her future submissions to producers and competitions. Just as mock interviews are excellent practice for landing your future dream job, being able to articulate the scope and commercial appeal of your screenplay and soliciting a professional's advice forms a good foundation for future pitch sessions.

A copy of this form follows so you can start polishing the answers that will help your screenplay shine.

PRELIMINARY SCRIPT COVERAGE QUESTIONNAIRE

Client Name:

Address:

Phone Number: Best time to reach you:

E-mail Address:

Title of Project:

Type of Project: Screenplay   Novel   Theater Script

Genre:

Target Audience:

Is your project: Completed   In Progress

Logline:

Synopsis (100 words or less):

Is your material: Original   Adapted from another source

For films and plays only, what is your estimated production budget:

In 100 words or less, please describe what makes this story unique, timely, and commercial for today's market:

What specific areas do you feel you need the most assistance with?

What specific strengths do you feel you bring to this project?

Please list previous publishing/performance/production credits:

Anything else I should know about you?

CHAPTER 13 | THE ART OF CONVERSATION

For as many conversations as we engage in every day — and as many more as we eavesdrop on — it's not always easy to duplicate that kind of energy, flow, and realism in a screenplay. Why? Because in this craft we so love called Art Imitating Life, we forget that life can play itself out in real time whereas the art of a feature length film is restricted to a scant two hours. Conversations with our friends, lovers, and children which can meander endlessly until they finally get to a point are the kiss of death when translated verbatim to the screen.

Too often someone who would be better suited to writing novels or short stories tries to put words in the mouths of live actors. It's a dead giveaway when a writer doesn't know what he/she is doing. Why? Because (1) the characters all talk exactly the same way, (2) they talk more eloquently than normal people, or (3) they talk way too much.

By simply learning to be a better listener, you can make your characters better conversationalists. This chapter shows you how.

THE SEDUCTION OF SOUND

Stand-up comics have long known that words containing g's, k's, p's, and q's are funnier than other words, especially if they're also coupled with repetition and shuffled letters (i.e., bass ackwards). Romance novelists rely heavily on words that begin with sl's, sm's, wh's and plenty of oo's (literally and figuratively) in the middle. One needs only to observe the lips/tongue action intrinsic to these combinations to see why they're so often used.

Technical writers, on the other hand, prefer multisyllabic words that favor b's, d's, r's, and Latin suffixes. There's an off-putting hardness and complexity to scientific dissertations because — well, quite frankly, they're not *supposed* to be easily understood by regular, workaday people.

In concert with these common patterns is the power of short-vowel sounds versus long-vowel sounds. Consider the difference, for example, between Indiana Jones retorting, "Now you're just getting nasty" and "Now you're just getting mean." Though both of them ascribe inappropriate behavior to the enemy, the "ă" tone in the first one is harsher than the more soothing "ee" sound in the second. Accordingly, which one packs more punch? Never use a limp word when a stronger/sexier/funnier one would be more potent. And don't forget that the physical order of lines not only impacts cadence but weight. Compare:

"My mother was a hooker. You go with what you've got."

"You go with what you're got. My mother was a hooker."

DELIVERY TIMES

Have you ever noticed that villains communicate more slowly and seductively than those who are trying to thwart them? Their time-clocks, after all, are completely different from those of the protagonists; they have the luxury of an *adagio* pace because, presumably, they are entirely too smart to be caught up with and, thus, have an ample head start.

Meanwhile, the good guys are operating at *prestissimo* because their lives and Western Civilization depend on it. This is reflected in shorter words, shorter lines, and a lower level of abstraction. Villains often embroider their speech with analogies to classic literature, philosophy, and antiquities, as well. Again it's because they've had the free time to read up on all of this while the hero was busy just trying to round up a posse.

Vocal variation and tempo can best be illustrated with a home stereo system. If you happen to have one with a bass and treble digital display, compare the difference between an evening "mellow sounds" DJ and a caffeine turbo-charged one who hosts the morning commute. Enlist friends to tape-record one of your own scenes and *watch* it being played back. Not only are you striving for definitive pacing in the speech patterns of the characters but a melange of energy flow within the scenes themselves.

THE ART OF CROSS-TALK CHIT-CHAT

Dialogue is a dance in which both characters are simultaneously trying to lead. What keeps the audience fixated and alert is the fact that even what seems like casual chit-chat is an artful cross-talk in which (1) questions are answered with other questions and (2) answers contain subtext that fuel the fires of controversy. Skillful dialogue can also be likened to a vigorous tennis game where the objective is to keep the opponent off-balance by returning the ball as quickly as one receives it.

Insults fly, sarcasm sizzles, and sibling rivalry reigns supreme in The Lion In Winter, *a must-see film for those who want to improve their skills at snappy dialogue and verbal sparring.* (The Lion In Winter, Hayworth Productions, 1968)

As much as you want to keep your audiences on their toes, however, you don't want to confuse them by incorporating multiple ideas within one speech or scene. Let them absorb whatever it is they're supposed to learn in Conversation #1, then move on to Conversation #2, much like a progressive dinner allows the guests to savor and understand everything about the appetizers before they move on to the next house that's serving the soup or salad. Just as the sum of the entire meal addresses the central theme of hunger, the sum of interaction among your characters revolves around the resolution of the story's central question.

NOT WITHOUT PURPOSE

Film dialogue serves four main functions:

1. To reveal character,
2. To advance the plot,
3. To explain the past, and
4. To articulate feelings that can't be conveyed visually.

If your characters' conversations aren't accomplishing one or more of the above, cut them out! Unlike the rambling chatter we engage in every day with family and friends, "screen talk" needs to have a good reason to be there. Ideally, it also should serve more than just one purpose at a time.

For instance, let's say you have a protagonist who admits, "I've been terrified of the water — even wading pools — ever since I saw my cousin drown in the Hudson when I was a kid."

This line:

1. Reveals that he/she is vulnerable,
2. Suggests that water will make an unbidden appearance somewhere in this story and force the protagonist to confront his/her fears,
3. Explains the source of the fear, in addition to establishing familial and geographical connections, and
4. Expresses what otherwise only could be shown in a flashback.

POETRY IN MOTION

One of the things I've noticed in my work as a coverage consultant is that younger writers per se, have a harder time mastering the art of cadence than writers of my own generation. Why? Because the study of poetry in public schools has significantly waned over the past 25 years. Anyone who has ever struggled to rhyme just the right word to fit a specific metre is head and shoulders above the "lyrically challenged" who are averse to massaging their prose for flow and economy.

If a character's monologue doesn't trip smoothly off the tongue, try to approach it as if it were a poem or a song. Once you've crafted the syncopated version of what you want to say, substitute selected words or phrases with others that contain the same number of syllables. For example:

> You told me it was just a lark
> This complicated mess
> And yet your car was double-parked
> Outside that slut's address.

VANESSA

You told me it was just a fling. You
begged me to forgive. And then I
see you—big as life—outside that
slut's address!

THE CRITICAL DOs AND DON'Ts OF DIALOGUE

Be wary of the Party Syndrome. This is the phenomenon whereby writers feel compelled to painstakingly have their characters come into a room for the first time and get introduced to everyone else who is already there. Unless it actually *is* a party or meeting where such introductions would be natural, find other ways to convey their identities to your audience. Try this baker's dozen for variety:

> Office phone calls (either outgoing or incoming)
> Name tags (for those in service professions)
> Office titles on doors
> Reservations at a restaurant
> Parties/business scenarios whereby introductions are natural
> Third-party remarks prior to arrival
> CUs of correspondence opened by addressee
> Speaking engagements in which he/she is introduced to a group
> Soliloquies where characters talk to themselves (use sparingly)
> VOs which book-end the film or run continuously throughout
> Job interviews or blind-date set-ups

> Paging (effective in hospital scenes)
> Newspaper/magazine match-cuts.

Avoid long monologues unless they're pertinent to the character or plot. If a character has something lengthy to say, break it up with interruptions from his/her listeners or bits of business/action. One of the analogies I like to use in workshops relates to the selection process by which people read magazine and newspaper articles. Are you more likely to be attracted to one which is a series of short paragraphs or one which goes on and on without any discernible breaks? Prospective producers read things the same way, preferring the readability of bite-size dialogue chunks and lots of white space.

Are your characters talking more to each other or to the audience as a contrivance to "fill them in?" Never let your characters explain things in explicit detail to each other that, presumably, they each already know.

Speaking of realism, always enlist an impromptu "cast" to read your scenes out loud after you have written them. This will reveal:
> If your sentences are so long that the actors could not conceivably take a big enough breath to deliver them.
> If you've used too many "s's" or combinations that make for outrageous tongue-twisters.
> If you've accounted for the fact that most people speak in fragments, use slang, and get interrupted.
> If you've used words to convey what could be better communicated through body language and facial expressions.
> If you've used phrases which look perfectly fine in print but which, if spoken, would cast a different meaning? The following lines were taken from actual scripts some of my students turned in. Read them out loud and you'll see what I mean:
"Running Bear will keep you safe."
"The prints showed me something I'd never seen before."
"I'm used to being chased."

"Uranus is really underrated."

"The boos drowned out my speech."

"Have you seen my beau?"

"I was nearly killed by a boar."

"If we're quick, we can catch a ferry."

"I need all the seamen you can give me."

"We got back to the zoo but it was too late. The rhino had already been poached."

AND FINALLY, A WORD ABOUT DIALECTS

Voracious reader that I am, there were quite a few pages of *Gone with the Wind* that I opted to skip when it first fell into my hands in high school. No, it wasn't because I wanted to see what Scarlett and Rhett would do next (oh, all right, maybe it was *partly* because of that). Nor was it because I already knew how the Civil War came out and thought all of the expositional battle scenes were tedious.

The real reason is that I got vexed with the phonetically illustrative Southern dialect because it slowed the momentum, forcing me to concentrate on the pronunciation of individual words instead of the flow of emotions being evoked. That same vexation surfaced years later when I encountered Diana Gabaldon's Scottish time-travel novels about the star-crossed lovers, Jamie and Claire. Passionate as I am about Highland history (I got married in a Scottish castle), the author's good intentions to capture the texture of a good brogue became cumbersome when spread over too many pages.

This may seem like an odd remark coming from someone who not only spent two decades in theater but learned to master a number of useful and/or exotic dialects in the process. Wouldn't I *want* to know how to convincingly mimic a foreign tongue? As an actress, yes. As a reader, no. And readers are generally the ones who will have the first look at your script.

Rather than slog down the pace by trying to phonetically capture the pronunciation of foreign/regional characters in your script, concentrate on their colloquial expressions and speech patterns instead. Above all, be *consistent* if you're attempting a style of lingo that differs from the one you were born with. Nothing looks worse than going from, "Yo, Theo, whassup, bro?" on the first page to the same character remarking three pages later, "I don't believe we've been properly introduced to one another."

CHAPTER 14 | VERBATIM AD NAUSEUM AND THE CURSE OF ADVERBS

Does size matter?

If your script is in the hands of an independent producer or studio scriptreader, you bet it does! In fact, their practice of flipping to the back page before they ever start reading can impact whether your script gets read at all. While a story that clocks in at less than 90 minutes can possibly be fluffed out or salvaged as a short, anything over two hours is automatically suspect as "too wordy."

If you're lucky enough to get feedback on *where* particular cuts can be made, take advantage of it. The majority of the time, however, you'll only be advised that the script is too long and be left to your own devices to figure out how to trim it down.

In my own experience as a script consultant, the "page-gobblers" tend to fall into five categories, all of which are easily remedied:

> Extraneous conversation (addressed in the previous chapter)
> Explicit character description
> Excessive scene description
> Calling too many shots
> Counting every step

CHARACTER DEFINING MOMENTS
A lot of writers — myself included — find it useful to have real life individuals in mind as models for the fictional characters who will people their screenplays. It can be a specific person, a facet of the author's own persona, or a composite of multiple personalities rolled into one. Maybe during the creative process they even go so far as to envision the celebrity "dream cast" they'd like to see act in it

and, accordingly, write lines and actions that would be the most suitable to those actors' talents and ages.

The plus side of this practice is that it helps keep characters and their speech patterns distinct from one another, especially if there are quite a few to keep track of. There's no mixing up which one is Jerry and which one is Clyde, for instance, if Jerry and Clyde are actual people whose respective looks, accents, and habits are firmly locked in the writer's memory banks and/or reinforced through regular interaction.

The minus side is that you can write yourself into a box from which you can't be rescued.

Back in the days when I ran an acting company, this method of casting reversal in my playwriting was the product of concurrently teaching acting classes and having a steady pool of new talent crossing the threshold. Each time I began penning scripts for the next season, I would not only have decided in advance which newcomers were ready for a debut but also which members of past shows would work well with them. As a result, I'd find myself purposely writing roles for players pre-cast in my head as opposed to the more traditional approach of holding structured auditions and making decisions based on who showed up.

Could other thespians have played those scenes with an equal amount of panache and credibility? Possibly. Unbeknownst to me at the time, however, I was limiting the chances of finding that out by so narrowly tailoring the roles to specific actors in my immediate company. To no great surprise, the only remaining theatrical scripts from those years which remain unsold to this day are the very same ones I had written for a young man named Billy whose proficiency with impersonations ranging from Kermit the Frog to Darth Vader went unmatched for 8+ years of production. It's not that the scripts were bad; they just needed a succession of leads like Billy to show them at their best.

Therein lies a common problem faced by new screenwriters who, in wanting to be exacting and precise in defining character traits, unwittingly jeopardize the discovery of whether a different spin might have brought something richer to the table. While Hollywood history is replete with memorable parts that we simply can't imagine anyone other than the original actor playing, it will diminish your first script's chances of a sale if you can't write parts with a broad degree of latitude.

In each of the following examples, certain characteristics have been ascribed to each of the characters in their first appearances on screen. See if you can identify which ones are essential in terms of projecting a certain type, as well as which ones lend themselves to substitution and/or omission.

> ANN, an exceptionally homely woman of 37, wears her dark brown hair in a bun and reading glasses on a bright red chain around her neck. She has on a flower print polyester dress from Target and a granny square sweater that her favorite aunt made for her.

> Two THIEVES run past an alley where a homeless man named LARRY is passed out in front of a green dented dumpster. Larry, a former state worker, is 55 and has scraggly grey hair in a ponytail, hazel eyes, a British accent, and a mole on the left side of his bulbous nose.

> MARTY just turned 33 last month but is still living his life as an extension of high school. His jet black hair is spiked and heavily gelled. He wears a pair of John Lennon wireframes, not because his apple green eyes are bad but because he thinks they make him look cool. He wears jeans with the knees ripped out, a Grateful Dead tee-shirt, and a pair of brand new Nike tennis shoes.

> GWEN is a 5' 9" career executive in her mid-40s with a Princess Diana hairstyle, piercing blue eyes, and a size 6 figure. Her only imperfection is a slight gap between her sparkling front teeth.

How did you do? Let's take a look.

AGE

Keep your references to age as generic as possible. Given the fact that a lot of actors and actresses pride themselves on the wide age-range they can physically play, the specificity of labeling someone as a "19-year-old coed" or "a 37-year-old drunk" could preclude those performers who fall on either side of those numbers from being called to audition. More importantly, providing a precise age may throw off a prospective producer or director whose vision of that particular character is different from yours. Use, instead, the terms "toddler," "teen," "young adult," "middle aged," etc., or refer to characters by the decade in which they would most comfortably fall for the sake of the plot; i.e., "twenties," "forties," "eighties," and so forth.

HAIR COLOR AND STYLE

Unless there is a familial relationship, an identity/fashion statement being made, or a dialogue reference to what is atop someone's head (i.e., "From the red of it, I'm guessing you're Irish" or "Did you grab the eggbeater instead of a hairbrush this morning?"), hair color and styling have nothing to do with the actual role. A bimbo, for instance, could just as easily be played by a brunette as a stereotypical blond. Whether a banker parts his hair on the left, the right, or is completely bald has no bearing on his ability to handle money. Apply that same logic to describing your characters' folicles.

In the examples given, the color of Ann's hair isn't as important as the unflattering style that she has chosen for it. Likewise, Marty's gel and spike look bespeaks an attachment to his wild-side youth but the exact hue is irrelevant. In addition, identifying a style in terms of a persona who popularized it only works if that style stayed the same for long enough to become a tag that will be easily understood by whoever reads the script. A reference to Princess Diana, for instance, conjures a universally consistent image; Jennifer Aniston and Cher, on the other hand, do not.

EYES

Unless the part calls for a specific eye color, don't bother to assign one... especially to characters like the homeless Larry whose eyes aren't even *open*!

CLOTHING AND ACCESSORIES

Minimize the use of specifics (i.e., colors, patterns, textures) and name brands in outfitting your players on paper. (I have actually had clients who itemized every single item of clothing in spite of the fact that none of it had anything to do with the plot or the persona wearing it!)

There are three exceptions to this guideline where a certain level of costuming detail is important:

> Trademark. In *Legally Blond*, the heroine's affinity for Barbie-style designer ensembles is used as an extension of how her personality is perceived by those around her. A narrowly defined wardrobe, thus, can be a tool to either validate an audience's assumptions regarding "type" or to mislead them with an external image that runs contrary to internal values.

> Clarity. What would Indiana Jones be without that manly and well-traveled fedora? To just say, "Indy is wearing a hat" invites multiple interpretations. Would he have cut the same swath in a snappy white boater? A sombrero? A bowler? In those instances where your intent could be misconstrued to the disadvantage of the character, spell out exactly what you want.

> Metamorphosis. Cher's dowdy duds and matronly hair in the first-half scenes of her Academy Award-winning *Moonstruck* role provide a startling contrast to the glamorous, second-half makeover she undergoes for her date at the opera with Nicholas Cage. In this case, the transformation in appearance symbolically coincides with the character's liberation from a previously dull and unsatisfying existence.

Is it significant that Marty is sporting a Grateful Dead tee-shirt instead of one for Smashing Pumpkins? What about the expensive Nikes which look out of place against his otherwise impoverished appearance? Is Marty an aspiring athlete who spends whatever extra cash he gets on the best sports footwear that money can buy? Did he steal those shoes from someone else and is flaunting them? Is he the only son in a wealthy family who likes to look radical just to freak out his parents? If you're going to introduce incongruities in your character's outward trappings, make sure you have a reason for it.

How about Ann? Two items in her ensemble are cause for curiosity. Is that granny square sweater a testament to bad taste or sentimentality? Unless the rest of Ann's closet is exposed to us over the course of the movie, we don't really know. And what about that bright red chain that holds her glasses, its color almost a show of defiance in the midst of drabness? Now that we've noticed it, what's it doing there? Further, the details of the dress she is wearing ("flower print polyester") are unnecessary; to simply say that it is "plain" or "cheap" is all that a reader—or costume coordinator—needs to know.

OTHER ITEMS TO OMIT
> Monikers 'R' Us. If a role is written in as simply part of the scene's general ambiance, he or she doesn't need to be assigned a name (i.e., the homeless gentleman has no lines, nor is he addressed by the other characters in conversation). At the same time, don't confuse a script reader by initially identifying characters by gender or occupation (in this case, THIEVES) and then attach names to them later on in the script. For example: "Enter JOE and MIKE, whom we recognize as the pair of thieves from page 5."
> Accents. In my work as a script coverage consultant, I'm always amused by references to characters who are described as "fussy Brits, articulate Germans, and suave Frenchmen"... and yet don't say a peep for the entire scene. If you're not going to allow them to open their mouths, assigning a specific dialect to them just doesn't make any sense.

> Attractiveness quotient. "Ann, an exceptionally homely woman..." Are there actually gradations of homeliness that we're not aware of? Stick to tags such as "plain," "handsome," "diamond in the rough," "drop dead gorgeous." And is it really essential that Gwen is a size 6 or that she has a Lauren Hutton smile? Not really. A size 9 with imperfect eyebrows could probably play the part just as well.

> Extraneous explanations. Avoid background data that we don't need to know. The origin of Ann's dress, for instance, or Larry's former occupation. If it's not going to be revealed via dialogue or action, it doesn't need to be explained in the description.

> Thought bubbles. Finally, don't embed inner thoughts within character profiles. If Marty wears John Lennon glasses because he associates John Lennon with coolness, let this come out in the context of the story itself. If this *isn't* a crucial facet of Marty's psyche, any pair of glasses — or lack thereof — would suffice.

WHEN LESS IS MORE

Back in grade school, we were all taught that adverbs and adjectives were our new best friends, enabling us to enrich our descriptions of people, places, and things. Certainly in novels and short stories, modifiers that lock down a specific hue or express a relation to time, manner, or degree help paint a vivid picture in the mind's eye.

In screenwriting, however, the opposite is true. The more you try to tell actors how to deliver their lines, set designers what color the furniture should be, or cinematographers how to point their cameras, the less they are going to like you... or your script.

FADE IN: EXT. /ROCKY MOUNTAIN MEADOW/DAY
The sound of a reddish-brown hawk pierces the tran-
quility of a lovely spring afternoon in the American
Rockies. The flawless azure sky has been lovingly
caressed by the painter's brush with wisps and
swirls of cotton-candy clouds that look down on a
crescent of sturdy verdant trees from which the forest's wildlife cautiously emerges, wary of Man's
presence in what was once their exclusive paradise.
An unseasonably warm breeze of 5 miles an hour sen-
sually ripples through the amber grasses, gently
parting them as if they were fluid gold and abrupt-
ly disturbing a family of bees which angrily spirals
upward like a miniature, bee-colored cyclone. Just
then, the camera gracefully pans leftward to two
riders on horseback who leisurely emerge upon the
scene, their faces bronzed and ruddy as a result of
long months in the wilderness. The animals pick up
their manly scent and, with noses twitching, quickly recede into the welcome protection of the shad-
ows. The first man, JEB KIMBRO, is in his late 20s,
blond and very handsome. The other man, CLAY ADAMS,
is about 40 with a hook-shaped nose and dark hair
parted roguishly on the side.

                    JEB
               (very grimly)
          It's quiet here.

                    CLAY
               (nods solemnly, slowly
               scratching his chin)
          Too quiet.

"But you keep telling me that film is *visual*," my client protested when I reduced
his opening scene to the following:

```
FADE IN: EXT. - ROCKY MOUNTAIN MEADOW - DAY
SFX: Hawk

SFX: Hoofbeats
Two frontiersmen, JEB KIMBRO and CLAY ADAMS, ride
into view.
```

Clearly his interpretation that movies need to be visually compelling was taken to mean that it's the writer's job on paper to leave no angstrom of detail to chance. Further, that by building as much narrative glitz (and all that bee-colored imagery) into the script as possible will increase its chances of sale.

On both counts, the answer is "no."

Why? Because a common mistake that new screenwriters make when crafting their stories is in forgetting who is actually going to be *reading* it and judging its merits. No, it's not the "target audience" for whom the film is intended, as their approval won't even come into play until the finished product reaches the box office. Instead, it's the "target director/producer" whose heart and imagination have to be won in the initial review, a quest which will be instantly defeated as soon as The Writer implies that The Reader has no sense of creativity.

SELF-TEST

In the scene with Jeb and Clay, go through the text and circle every adverb and every adjective that you can find. Quite a few, hmm? Now go back and identify which ones are necessary to the scene. Of the original total you came up with, what percentage of these were actually relevant?

Now take a page from your own script and do the same thing. The lesson to be learned here is to use adverbs and adjectives sparingly. A good rule to follow is that if you have more than six per page, you are probably going into more detail that you need.

While there are obvious occasions where a certain level of definition is required to address ambiguity (i.e., a *Martha Stewart* cabin versus a *crude* cabin), it's important to ask yourself just how wedded you are to a particular likeness, representation, or camera shot before you commit it to paper. Unlike a novel or short story, in which you are illustrating a character, location, or action sequence as accurately as possible for a passive audience, the words of a film or television script are simply the *framework* on which the directing, acting, and technical talent will build outward and embellish with their own signature styles.

In fairness to my student, of course, I should point out that his justification for being "visually wordy" came from an assignment I had given him to download some scripts from *www.scriptdude.com* and familiarize himself with both the formatting and "cinema shorthand" which separates amateurs from professionals. One of the examples he cited in his defense was excerpted from the award-winning *Braveheart* by Randall Wallace:

```
EXT. THE SCOTTISH COUNTRYSIDE—DAY.
Epic beauty. Cobalt mountains beneath a glowering
purple sky fringed with pink, as if the clouds were
a lid too small for the earth; a cascading landscape
of boulders shrouded in deep green grass; and the
blue lochs, reflecting the sky.
```

"If Mel Gibson didn't have a problem with the way it was written," my student protested, " why can't I get away with the same thing?"

The short answer is that, well, Life isn't fair. The longer answer is that, well, I don't think Mel knows who you are (yet).

Herein lies an important distinction for new writers who use downloaded scripts as a guide for writing their own. For screenwriters who have already established themselves in the industry and/or a financial commitment or talent attachment has already been made for this particular script, liberties can be taken in the writing that newcomers just can't get away with. (Movies produced by James Cameron are another good example of this.)

To break into the system and eventually become one of those people who can do whatever they want requires that you adhere to the rules at the outset, the primary rule being, "Don't direct on paper." Your job as the writer is simply to tell the story, people it with unforgettable characters, and leave the swirls of insect cyclones and azure skies to the vision and discretion of the experts.

AND THEN WE'LL MOVE THE CAMERA OVER HERE....

In earlier books on the craft of screenwriting, it was a popular practice to encourage the use of camera shots and angles throughout the script. Not only did this use up a lot of space but made scripts cumbersome to read.

For instance:

```
WIDE ANGLE on ESTHER and MELVIN.
CU of Melvin, waving.

                    MELVIN
              Hey, Esther!

CUT TO:
MEDIUM SHOT of Esther, looking around

CUT TO:
Melvin POV.

DISSOLVE TO:
LONG SHOT of Esther as a child.
TRAVELING SHOT as Melvin moves toward her.

                    ESTHER
              Oh my God!

CUT TO:
MEDIUM SHOT of Esther turning to run away from
Melvin.
```

```
CUT TO:
Esther POV crashing through the woods.
CU of Melvin, out of breath.

CUT TO:
AERIAL SHOT of the chase.
```

Screenwriting texts today have taken the opposite approach, recommending that camera directions be used sparingly. That includes the often liberal use of the phrase "cut to" when used to switch to a different scene. Nor should you number your master scenes, as these numbers will have no relevance when the whole thing is turned into a shooting script.

WE'RE WALKING, WE'RE TALKING, WE'RE MAKING A SEGUE

Moving film characters from one venue to another is something that seems to stymie new writers. As a result, they err on the side of playing out transitions in real time rather than simply cutting to the next point of action.

For instance, let's say that co-workers Cindy and Allison have decided to go to lunch. The novice screenwriter would show them:
> Going to their respective cubicles to get their purses
> Putting on their coats
> Going into the hallway
> Pressing the elevator call button
> Riding in the elevator
> Getting out on the first floor
> Exiting the building
> Walking to the corner
> Waiting for the traffic signal to change to "Walk"
> Crossing the street
> Walking seven blocks....

We can only hope these two have a really long lunch hour for as much time as it's going to take them to reach the restaurant. It would be one thing, of course, if their noon-time journey were fraught with peril in the form of Ninjas, high-speed chases, a typhoon, and a runaway trolley. Even if the walk itself were a device to reveal character quirks (i.e., Allison never steps on cracks) or peel off another layer of the plot (i.e., Cindy divulges that she is sleeping with the CEO), its circuitous nature as currently written would take up more pages than a two-hour movie can afford to spend.

A better approach, which cuts to the chase, would be:

```
INT. CINDY'S OFFICE - LUNCHTIME
Allison pops her head in, sees Cindy engrossed in
work. She knocks on the door. Cindy looks up,
startled to see her.

                    CINDY
          Oh shit! Were we—

                    ALLISON
          Uh-huh.

Cindy scrambles to get her purse.

                    CINDY
          I swear to God, it totally
          slipped my mind.

                    ALLISON
          You want to know what I
          think?

INT. - RESTAURANT - LATER
The two friends are halfway through their Cobb salads.

                    CINDY
          Seriously?

                    ALLISON
          Is this the face of a
          woman who lies?
```

```
                    CINDY
          It's the face of a woman who
          can't step on cracks.
          Jeez-Louise, you're blowing
          the whole thing out of
          proportion. Rick and I are
          just friends.

                    ALLISON
          Just friends, huh?
```

Without having to spend a lot of time in transition, this example gets to the gist of the Allison/Cindy dialogue and keeps the plot moving forward.

This same sense of scripting brevity should be applied to scenes in which the actors are required to engage in fight sequences... or in eating. Oddly enough, these are the two occasions when newbies feel compelled to spell out *every single movement*. In a bar-room brawl, for example, they go to great lengths describing whether the punch is done with the left or right fist, how many bobs and weaves are done by either side, and which foot the opponent steps back on before he crashes, bloody and battered, to the tavern floor. Because these scenes will be carefully choreographed by experts in order to avoid injuries, it isn't necessary for the screenwriter to account in print for each blow. Simply say, "they fight" and leave the specifics to the pros.

In restaurant scenes, the one page equals one minute rule is put to two extreme tests. In the first, the diners are shown to their table, given menus, place their orders, have those orders delivered, and then announce, "We should be getting back" — all in the space of about 45 seconds! In the second instance, I have a number of clients who go so far as to write in directions such as: Picks up fork, takes a bite of potatoes, switches fork to left hand and picks up knife with right, slices a piece of steak, chews thoughtfully, etc., etc., etc. Simply say, "they eat" and leave the specifics to the performers. Trust me. I have yet to meet a starving actor who didn't know what to do with a plate of food in front of him.

CHAPTER 15 | FOREIGN EXCHANGE OR WHAT MAKES YOU THINK THEY'RE GOING TO LIKE THIS ANY BETTER IN CANADA?

"My plot is dark and sort of creepy," the writer explained. "It probably won't appeal to American audiences, so maybe you can use your contacts in the United Kingdom and try to sell it for me over there."

The assumption that a project which hasn't yet ignited within U.S. borders will suddenly become a house afire overseas is one that, unfortunately, a lot of new writers seem to embrace. Certainly the encouragement of seeing fledgling rock groups from Bakersfield take Tokyo by storm or soap star extras stealing the limelight in Eastern European indies has fueled the conclusion that foreigners will buy virtually anything with an Uncle Sam label.

Wrong.

No matter the product, it still has to be good to begin with.

The aforementioned story — a poorly stitched consolidation of themes liberally borrowed from *Les Miserables*, *Paper Moon*, *David Copperfield*, and *Annie* — was intended to expose a secret that most of us were probably already aware of: 1840s London wasn't a very pleasant place to be if you were an orphan in a work-house run by cruel overseers.

"British audiences will like it," the author insisted, "because I've really captured the way things were." The phonetic dialects, she further explained, were the product of years of renting English videos and copying down all of the nuances.

I felt compelled to point out another fallacy in the strategy of mimicking accents in order to impress readers who were born with real ones. Just as the French can easily differentiate their own native speakers from even the most fluent graduates of Berlitz, so, too, can the nationals of other countries recognize when someone is appropriating their culture, history, and speech patterns in order to pen a trendy script.

I had encountered a similar situation myself in doing the initial research for a musical on Princess Kaiulani. "Haoles (non-Hawaiians)," I was informed, "have no understanding of what it is to accurately capture the essence of Hawaii." Impassioned as a writer can be about a particular topic, it takes more than surface imitation to give a story credible depth.

My client continued to assert that her work would be lauded as illustrating just how horrible, filthy, unscrupulous, and debauched the Englishmen (and women) of the time could be when it came to the treatment of defenseless children.

"And these," I queried, "are the same people you want to sell to?"

While this should not, of course, limit an author to just writing about his or her backyard, it does call to the fore the need for diplomacy when condemning the denizens of the very market you'd like to break into. It's one thing, as they say, for relatives to trash their own but woe to the outsider who steps in and attempts to do the same.

In keeping with the theme of courting foreign publishers, film producers, and theater companies, the following guidelines can make all the difference between making a sale and making an enemy.

UNDERSTAND THE COMPETITION

Just because your plot has been rejected by everyone you've sent it to in the U.S. doesn't mean it will be gobbled up by a "lesser" entity abroad. The argument that foreign buyers ascribe to lower standards in evaluating creative material is completely unfounded. If anything, the rules are even *more* strict, given the fact that publishing and performance preference will be given to the writers who hail from their own countries first. As an outsider, your work not only needs to be bulletproof in terms of quality and professionalism but must make enough of an impression to rise above the talents of the existing local competition.

Nor should you assume that because a particular genre is so saturated and over-done in the American market that you can go hawk it to foreigners who don't know any better. One needs only to look at distribution sales in paperbacks, videos, and Internet merchandising to realize that our global neighbors are just as abreast of entertainment trends as we are and — like everyone else — are looking for The Next New Thing.

THE COLOUR/COLOR OF MONEY

Whether your objective is to sell a magazine filler or a feature-length film, it pays to study the spelling, colloquialisms, and metric conversions of your targeted market before you submit your material. This accomplishes two things, both of which will endear you to a buyer. The first is a demonstration of having done your homework and learning what your virtual host considers to be "correct" usage. Too often, the arrogance with which a writer insists that everyone else is "spelling it incorrectly" results in a failed opportunity to make a sale.

Likewise, the liberal use of American slang either poses a barrier to user-friendly understanding or suggests a meaning that wasn't intended (i.e., "We didn't have dessert because we were stuffed"). The second perk to abiding by foreign rules of usage is the amount of time an editor perceives he or she ultimately will save in having to edit the finished product. It's easier to say yes to a work that requires little revision than one that assumes knowledge on the part of the reader or projects an ethnocentric superiority.

ENLISTING FOREIGN AID

When I began penning *The Missionary Position*, a stage comedy set in Australia, I thought the dialogue would be fairly easy. As a fan of Paul Hogan movies and a devotee of that wacky croc hunter, Steve Irwin, the liberal inclusion of "Crikeys," "Mates," and "Sheilas" seemed enough to capture the indomitable and fun-loving spirit and candor of the Aussies.

Fortunately, I had the wits to share the script-in-progress with one of my associates in Adelaide before I submitted it into competition. "None of the rest of us talk like that," she informed me, generously offering to go through the lines and "Aussie-ize" them for me. The play went on to win an award, something that would not have happened without the two cents of a native-born expert.

This fact continues to be brought home as my list of foreign clientele steadily grows, the single biggest request for assistance being in the area of "Americanizing" the conversations. The best advice I give in that regard is something that I happily credit to the VietNamese manicurists in the salon where I get my nails done: watch soap operas. The longevity of this genre — whether it's in the U.S. or overseas — provides a training in dialogue that you simply can't get from a class. Not only are the topics universal in nature but are delivered in a slow, articulate manner that enables those who are trying to mimic dialect, cadence, or "status" nuances to follow.

STAMP OUT LAZINESS

While the Internet has been a huge bonus to those of us who grew up having to affix envelopes with sufficient return postage for our submissions, there are still markets in the world that do business by Snail Mail. There are also authors who assume that any country (1) sharing a border with the U.S. (Canada, for instance) or (2) sharing the same language (England, for example) uses U.S. stamps. Wrong. If you're mailing a script overseas and would like a reply, you have the following options: (1) International Reply Coupons, which are subsequently traded at the recipient's post office for the requisite amount of first class stamps, (2) Internet purchases of foreign postage, or (3) befriending a fellow foreign writer who is just as zealous about getting American stamps and setting up your own "swap meet."

Finally, there is the popular alternative of simply requesting that any communications regarding the project be sent to you via e-mail. You won't get your submission returned, of course, but considering the length and path of the journey it would have to take anyway to wing its way home, you might just be better off saving that return postage and printing out a fresh copy for the next pair of eyes that will see it.

CUSTOMARY HOMEWORK

Last but not least, make sure that you're targeting the right market for your work in terms of timeliness, social relevance, and universal truths. You wouldn't, for instance, zero in on India as a top buyer for your documentary on "Beef: It's What's for Dinner." Nor would you send your R-rated screenplay to an independent production company in Germany whose past credits have all been after-school specials on famous composers. Not only are such scatter-gun tactics a waste of money but a demonstration that you haven't bothered to research the buyer's needs, interests, or current trends.

To use a romance analogy, would you rather receive a Valentine that spoke specifically to you and, accordingly, made you feel as if you were singled out for special attention or one which was xeroxed and had all the prior recipients' names scratched off? When you're courting a prospective match for your submission either at home or abroad, nothing less will do than identifying all the things you have in common, playing to your strengths, and — oh yes — speaking their language, metaphorically and otherwise.

SCOPING OUT FOREIGN MARKETS

> Familiarize yourself with what is being produced overseas. Watch the credits at the end of foreign films and develop a matrix of recurring themes and genres within the various production companies.
> Read the trades. International film magazines and newsletters are where you'll find interviews with directors and production staff. Not only do they discuss their current and upcoming

movie projects, but oftentimes yield insight into favorite causes, pet peeves, and early beginnings.

> Foreign Film Commissions. Just like state film commissions that exist throughout the United States, foreign countries have comparable agencies that facilitate the workings of imported and exported movies. To do an Internet search, type in the name of the country you'd like to research. For instance, "Scottish Film Commission" or, in a broader sense, "United Kingdom Film Commissions."

> Bookmark the Internet Movie Data Base at *www.imdb.com*. Not only does it have an art house/international films tab and interviews with foreign producers, but also a section related to international film festivals.

> A number of screenwriting Web sites include entries from foreign producers seeking to tap international talent banks. Here are a few to get you started:

MovieBytes
www.moviebytes.com

Backstage.com
www.backstage.com

DV Café
www.dvshop.ca

BSP Live
www.bsplive.com/ScriptsWanted.html

Scriptseeker
www.scriptseeker.com/callboard.html

The Source
www.thesource.com.au

Keep in mind, of course, that priority tends to be given to those screenwriters who reside in the same country as the production company that is soliciting scripts. Contracts negotiated will also be subject to the industry laws and regulations of that country, as well as the employment fees paid and taxes collected for specified services.

CHAPTER 16 | HOW TO PROTECT YOUR PLOTS

Before that masterpiece script ever leaves your sight, you need to take the appropriate steps to ensure no one tries to steal it. This chapter explains the basics of how to do that.

FORGET THE POOR MAN'S COPYRIGHT

Gathering dust in hall closets across America are probably plenty of self-addressed envelopes bulging with manuscripts that the authors were either too lazy or too cheap to officially register as original material. As proof of authenticity, this practice known as "the poor man's copyright" would legally hold up in court.

The question is, though, why run the risk of tearing that envelope open by accident or misplacing it altogether when the procedures to establish ownership and date of completion are so easy?

Furthermore, over half the screenwriting contests you'll ever enter — not to mention the number of markets you'll want to submit your work to — require that the material be registered prior to submission.

Here's where to do it and what it will cost, a small investment compared to what you would have to spend if your screenplay's originality was ever challenged.

U.S. COPYRIGHT OFFICE
http://www.copyright.gov
Once upon a time if writers wanted to call upon Uncle Sam to help them protect their creative projects from unscrupulous idea thieves, they had to send away to Washington D. C. for an information package and copious forms. Not

only did it take a long time to receive these materials by mail, but it took even longer to actually get manuscripts processed through the system.

The bad news is that it still takes a long time to receive a copyright certificate, even though the effective date of registration is the date that the application, the manuscript, and the fees are received for processing. On the brighter side, however, the Copyright Office can now save time at the front-end of the submission procedure by having all of the requisite forms accessible on-line, along with the most frequently asked questions regarding what copyright means. The $30 filing fee will protect your work for your lifetime plus 70 years thereafter.

Note: While you're certainly welcome to include the copyright symbol, ©, after your title, do not include the year of registration. "Dated" material puts forth an immediate bias that the content isn't "fresh."

WRITERS' GUILD OF AMERICA
http://www.wga.org
Registration with WGA is available to both members and non-members, and covers all stages of script development for radio, television, and feature films. In the event that legal action is ever initiated against a registered work, it is helpful to have had the submission date duly logged with the Guild as evidence of its origination. It should be noted that many screenwriting contests now require WGA registration as a prerequisite to participate. This registration is valid for five years and may be renewed for an additional five years. Cost to members is $10; nonmembers pay $20.

Note: Novice writers often include their Writers' Guild registration number on the front cover of their scripts. Don't.

FIRST USE
http:/www.firstuse.com
In a hurry to protect your new script, as well as get it quickly into public circulation? First Use is an innovative, international registration service which allows

writers to catalogue their work at any stage of development from synopsis to final product. This method of direct, online filing can be performed at the cost of only $10 (less for volume submissions), provides a verifiable paper-trail of progress, and remains in effect for 10 years.

PROTECT RITE
http://www.protectrite.com
Protect Rite is another online registration service which was established to protect intellectual properties. Treatments, drafts, and completed scripts created with any word-processing program can be submitted electronically to this site and placed in 10-year storage at the cost of $18.95. Once the received material is encrypted and filed, only the author has access to registration. Just as with First Use, participants are e-mailed confirmation receipts establishing the submission date of their material. It should also be noted that files cannot be modified or altered once they have been electronically filed with this service.

WRITE SAFE
http://www.writesafe.com
The WriteSafe Group was launched in 1999, is similar in scope to other electronic filing services, and offers a comparable price ($10 for initial filing/$15 for every two subsequent pieces). It also provides an optional publishing component whereby your work can be viewed by others. This may or may not be a practicality, depending on your needs. Although the electronic date stamp can prove when the work was first registered, the likelihood of a potential producer actually surfing the site for a hot new project is probably remote. On the other hand, the likelihood of someone else getting inspired and writing a different-but-suspiciously-similar adaptation of the same idea is pretty high.

For more information on copyright, trademarks, and whether it's okay to put Elvis in your latest flick, the following site provides a host of timely articles, as well as a question and answer component: *http://www.Hollywoodnetwork.com/law.*

Likewise, the Writers' Guild of America (*http://www.wga.org*) includes a free mentor section in which your screenwriting rights questions can be posted and answered by industry professionals.

A WARNING ABOUT WEB SITES

It used to be believed that if a company had business cards and professional-looking letterhead, it was obviously legitimate. After all, why would it have gone to the time and expense of investing in such lovely stationery if it were just a fly-by-night operation?

Suffice it to say, that investment in paper PR products is a small price to someone unscrupulous. After all, the amounts that can be brought in by preying on the gullibility of the public will not only be an easy return on their print-shop payment but quite a bit of long-term profit, as well.

I've been asked to mention this as a warning by nearly every professional who contributed his or her expertise to the making of this book. Internet Web sites have replaced letterhead and business cards as a powerful medium through which to attract new business... and new victims. Not a day goes by that we don't read in the paper about sting operations which reveal the identity of individuals pretending to be something or someone they're not in order to gain the trust of those with whom they correspond. The most prevalent, of course, are those which promise romance, masking the darker intentions of sexual predators, con artists, and those behind bars seeking some easy cash, sympathy, and a new place to call "home" when they get out.

While the lonely hearts category takes a lion's share of victims of *all* ages, the biggest bait for wannabe screenwriters resides in the category of "I Can Make You a Star." It's a con that works because of the "instant now" society in which we live. Whether one dreams of fame and fortune as a rock star, actor, model or scriptician, we don't want to have to wait for it to happen.

Who wouldn't be lured by Web sites that promise immediate delivery of our highest expectations, especially if they're accompanied by eye-popping graphics, interactive demos, and "testimonials" alluding to a close and personal relationship with Britney, Jennifer Lopez, Matt Damon, etc.

"You, too," they hint, "can join the in-crowd elite and be the envy of all your friends." The catch, of course, is that it means you'll have to part with some money up front ("good faith" is usually the excuse given) and/or act quickly because only a select few are being "invited" to participate in this opportunity to have their work — or themselves — discovered by talent scouts.

If an offer sounds too perfect to be true — well, there's a good reason for that. Success in anything rarely comes overnight but is, instead, the end result of years of hard work and persistence. Tempting as it may be to enter every contest and answer every cattle call for new scripts, learn to be discriminating about what you're getting into.

If it's an agency or production company, do your homework in finding out what — if anything — they have actually gotten produced. If it's a contest, who is sponsoring it and how many years has it been running? You'll also want to check out the *www.moviebytes.com* "report card" on screenwriting competitions, as well as post inquiries at screenwriter chatrooms. This is an industry in which word travels fast; if others have been burned by Internet scams, they're quick to get out the warning to their peers.

Last but not least, never sign a contract unless you have a thorough understanding of what the whole thing means.

SECTION 4

WINNING THEM OVER

CHAPTER 17 | ALL ABOUT AGENTS

If you were seeking a date for an upcoming social event, would you flip open a phone book and call the first name your pencil-point dropped on? Of course not! Yet many writers use the same technique when seeking agents to represent their screenplays.

Truth be told, there's actually a lot of similarity between courting a prospective film agent for your work and testing the waters of a new relationship. Specifically, (1) do you have enough in common to sustain a long-term association with one another, (2) were you introduced by someone who knows both of you, and (3) how do you get out of it, if it doesn't make you happy?

Time and again, I've counseled writers who have been so thrilled that someone has finally agreed to pay attention to them that they end up sabotaging themselves and/or tolerating all manner of shoddy treatment. Just like those who have been out of romantic circulation for awhile, their approach to reps is often nervous, desperate, and too unfocused to inspire confidence.

Herein are some guidelines for not only ensuring call-backs from the right people but heeding warning signals about the wrong ones. (If they work for your love life, too, consider it a bonus!)

MAKING THE RIGHT MATCH

Different agents represent different markets and genres. This enables them to establish a solid contact base, as well as bank on a good reputation. Studios, networks, and independent producers recognize that scripts which have crossed these agents' desks and have been forwarded for consideration are not only the cream of the crop but are in keeping with current trends and sensibilities.

That said, it's essential that you do your homework in researching the best agent to put in your corner. If you want to write romantic comedies, for instance, you need to seek out a rep who's familiar with that genre and knows whom to sell it to. Forget whatever you've heard about mailing a glut of query letters to everyone you can find. The only thing that a scatter-gun approach will get you is faster word-of-mouth that you're too lazy to tailor a submissions list.

There are also two different types of agencies. The one you have probably heard the most about is the literary or "boutique" agency. These organizations exist to serve the interests of the writer and are delineated by areas of specialization (i.e., fiction, non-fiction, theatrical scripts, screenplays, etc.). The job of the agent in this venue is to promote, pitch, negotiate, and oversee the author's project, as well as make recommendations on what that author should be doing next to advance his/her writing career.

A packaging or talent management agency represents writers, too, but in concert with the management of actors, directors, musicians, and producers. The agent's role in this type of operation is to pull together all the elements of a viable "team" and present it to a studio or network for a fee. Because they have access to all the necessary ingredients for a successful enterprise, the cost and time savings to a potential buyer can be enormous.

The advantages and disadvantages to both types of representation, of course, are dependent on what kind of relationship you want to establish — that of a big fish in a small pond or a small fish in a big pond.

Boutique agencies recognize that writers are gold. Accordingly, they work hard to nurture and develop a promising talent who will, hopefully, fulfill all of their expectations with a stream of steady hits. While it may take longer to orchestrate an option or sale, they enter relationships with the premise of grooming an author for literary stardom.

In contrast, a packaging agency is dealing with elements of the equation that, from their standpoint, inspire more jaw-dropping awe than you do. To them, the script itself is just a cog in a much larger wheel. While that's not to say that the wheel won't spin into some pretty exciting opportunities for you, there is already formidable competition in place before you ever walk in the door; specifically, a stable of experienced scripticians they keep on retainer to pen things in a jiffy for Russell Crowe or Angelina Jolie.

WHERE THE AGENTS ARE

> HOLLYWOOD REPRESENTATION DIRECTORY
   Publisher: Hollywood Creative Directory, April 2003

> DONE DEAL – Agents and Managers link
   www.scriptsales.com/Donedealagency.html

> WRITER'S MARKET – Script Agents Chapter
   Publisher: Writer's Digest Books (Annual publication, also available as CD-Rom)

> 2003 ANNUAL AGENCY GUIDE
   Publisher: Fade In, January 2003

> WRITERS NET: LITERARY AGENTS
   www.writers.net/agents.html

> WRITER'S GUIDE TO HOLLYWOOD PRODUCERS, DIRECTORS, AND SCREENWRITER'S AGENTS, 2002-2003: WHO THEY ARE! WHAT THEY WANT! AND HOW TO WIN THEM OVER!

> Publisher: Prima Lifestyles, June 2001

> WRITERS GUILD OF AMERICA
   www.wga.org

> 2003 GUIDE TO LITERARY AGENTS: 600+ AGENTS
  WHO SELL WHAT YOU WRITE By Rachel Vater
  Publisher: Writers Digest Books, November 2002

> SCREENWRITING ON THE INTERNET By Christopher
  Wehner
  Publisher: Michael Wiese Productions, 2001

STORM WARNINGS

Would you pursue someone who wasn't gainfully employed or was evasive about what he/she did for a livelihood? Would you raise an eyebrow of suspicion if they only wanted to meet you at doughnut shops or in alleys? Would you feel secure with people who had either (1) never sustained any long-term relationships, (2) blamed all past failures on other parties, or (3) couldn't remember any names because none of them stayed in the picture long enough?

What many people don't realize is that virtually anyone can hang out a shingle, throw together a Web site, and start calling himself an agent. While there are professional organizations and membership guilds that many reps belong to, it is not a mandatory requirement for conducting business, nor is a college degree or special license a prerequisite to hawking scripts.

Will your agent expect you to foot the bill for all of the postage, script photocopying, long distance phone calls, and wardrobes for schmoozing at Hollywood parties? Likewise, will you be expected to shell out large sums of money in order for your agent to keep telling you what a stellar writer you are?

These and other questions need to be asked before you enter a contractual agreement. This isn't the time to be shy about asking your prospective representative what, exactly, he or she has done in terms of actual sales and options. How long have they been in business? Do they provide written contracts that specify their terms and timeframes? How difficult or expensive will it be for you to extricate yourself from a liaison that doesn't seem to be going anywhere? If the rep belongs to an agency and decides to move to a different one, what provisions will be made for you as the screenwriter (i.e., will you be assigned to someone else at the original agency or will you be expected to tag along to the new address)?

Watch out for makeover artists, as well. How many times have you found yourself in the position of being besotted with someone who had a never-ending list of "improvements" you should make to yourself — a new hairdo, different clothes, revised viewpoints — only to be subsequently dumped for someone uncannily similar to whomever you were originally?

Agents can be just as judgmental. While constructive advice is always helpful in tweaking a diamond-in-the-rough script, beware of those who try to reshape your entire style to fit the limitations of their own sales abilities. Early in my book-writing career, I had such an agent who tried to turn every mainstream plot into a formulaic romance. Why? Because the romance market was the only one she knew how to sell to.

Always remember that even though an agent may have a map to get you to your star-studded destination, the car still belongs to you.

WHAT'S THE BUZZ

Screenwriters who have been burned by bad agents are always generous about sharing their experiences with others. One of the best places to read these "bewares" is Jenna Glatzer's excellent Web site: *www.absolutewrite.com/forum/index.html*.

INDUSTRY REFERRALS

Back in the 1970s, I often found myself coaxed into blind dates by well-meaning friends who thought I should be attached. I usually said yes, thinking that the odds of being hooked up with a loser were remote and that my friends knew me well enough to facilitate a few quality matches. The reality, of course, was that Mr. Right never materialized from any of these introductions, nor are any of these friends still in my address book.

Fortunately for those of you who are unattached screenwriters, the film business is a little more promising. The reason is that there is more at stake in the professional arena than around the water-cooler. For an industry expert to vouch for an author who has neither the product, the focus, nor the right attitude to be of value to a prospective agent translates to only one thing — a diminishment of trust. Even if the next "gem" is a match made in heaven, it only takes one dud to produce eyebrow-raising skepticism ever after.

One of the bonuses of third-party introductions, of course, is that a chemistry can ignite that might not have been discovered if the two individuals being matched had been left to their own devices. When someone knows the likes, dislikes, and objectives of both sides, who better to bring them together? At least a third of the interviews in this book, in fact, were the product of industry associates who remarked, "There's someone I'd like you to meet. I think you'd hit it off."

If you're fortunate enough to make useful connections, just be warned of three things you shouldn't do:
1. Assume that the outcome is going to be a success as a result of mutual association. The go-between is only a catalyst who got the ball rolling.
1. Blame the go-between if you get rejected. It's not his or her fault that you and your script just weren't what the other party happened to be looking for.
1. Embrace a breezy familiarity just because the contact is a friend-of-a-friend. This is a business-related introduction and should be treated as such until you're invited to take it to a different level.

NO MORE, NO LESS
One of the biggest complaints that agents make about prospective clients is the latter's tendency to send more than was what asked for. Certainly if a requested sample of 10 pages plus a synopsis is a promising sign of interest, wouldn't sending the entire manuscript be even better?

No.

The reason that reps ask for a specified amount of material is that their skills are honed to the point of being able to identify, in a relatively short sample, whether the rest of the story will be worth reading. To send more (and yes, it's a hard temptation to resist) not only tells the reader that you don't know how to follow simple instructions, but that you're arrogant enough to believe he or she will set everything else aside just because you sent the whole thing. In my own experience, I actually had someone pen the following note: "I know you told me you only wanted the first three chapters of my book, but I knew you would get hooked once you got started reading this and that you would lose sleep waiting for me to mail the rest of it."

Observing formalities also extends to the issue of whether it's better to send an e-mail query or a snail-mailed one. While the Internet has impacted the number of agents (and producers) who now accept electronic introductions, it's important that you take the time to find out what is the preferred approach.

It's also essential that your screenplay be completed before you start pitching it to prospective buyers. If it's only in the embryonic stage, an agent will not be interested in waiting around for you to finish it, no matter how good a story it may be.

Last but not least, never send a script — or even a portion of your script — unless it has been specifically requested. I guarantee you that unsolicited material will either be returned unopened, or deposited in the agency's nearest round file.

INTERVIEW WITH AN EXPERT
Want to know what Hollywood is looking for? Let's see what a top-ranked agent has to say.

Peggy Patrick, v.p. of television at Shapiro-Lichtman is the first woman to serve in this capacity in the 31-year history of the agency. Peggy oversees and directs the activities of the Television Department, which includes handling the careers of more than 200 working clients. She created and developed the Animation/Family and Children's Department and is recognized as one of the top agents in this arena.

Peggy currently represents writers, directors, and producers in all areas both in features and television. Martin Shapiro and Mark Lichtman founded the Shapiro-Lichtman Agency in 1969. The Agency currently represents approximately 400 clients including writers, directors, producers, below the line, and talent.

Let's start with the $64,000 question: what is Hollywood looking for?
Everything – In fact there are so many different markets now in Hollywood that they really are looking for everything. There are companies looking for big block-busters, companies looking for small "important" films. TV always wants big-event projects based on books or big news stories. There has been an upswing in people wanting romantic comedies lately. Big family comedies are in demand. People are always looking for the next High Concept. I would say that scripts more than pitches are selling right now. I guess what Hollywood is looking for is a really great story that millions of people will pay $10 a pop to see.

The proliferation of film-oriented Web sites and online script submission opportunities has dramatically increased the newcomer's accessibility to Hollywood. With writers now able to negotiate contracts directly with prospective producers, how has this impacted the role of today's agents?
Not at all – we are so overwhelmed with writers wanting us to look at their scripts that I figure if someone can do it himself or herself – GREAT. I haven't felt any slow down of writers trying to get me to represent them at this time. I also would caution writers who want to do it themselves – that just like in real estate – you better know what you are doing if you choose to negotiate your own deal. There are huge pitfalls – some that can be avoided and some that can't. On many occasions I have had people come to me when they were already in the midst of some deal that they had partially negotiated for themselves – and without exception they had messed up at many levels – and usually to the point of the problem not being able to be fixed.

In your view, are agents more crucial in the capacity of *getting* established or in *staying* established?

Staying established. Unfortunately it is almost impossible to get an agent if you haven't already gotten established.

In the publishing world, literary agents seek authors who can generate many commercial concepts as opposed to just one. Does the same hold true with film reps in their decision to take on new clients? In other words, is it the discovery of a single blockbuster script that excites you or the chance to foster a long-term relationship with a screenwriter who has multiple ideas up his or her sleeve?

I always want a long-term relationship. It could take years to find or get that blockbuster off the ground – after that, you want to keep building – it should only get better. Unfortunately what a lot of writers do is stay with one agent until their "ship comes in" in the form of some big movie and then they bolt for a bigger agency – only to disappear into the masses again. That's because the person who probably got them to that point really put the energy in and had the passion to get them there – and some other bigger agency really is surprised when the next script isn't perfect or selling, etc., and it drops the writer. Relationship is important. You want agents who believe in you when you're small and they want you to remember them when you are big. Unfortunately that is not always the case.

What are some of the biggest mistakes you see in a novice screenwriter's approach to securing professional representation?

Being too cute or wordy in the query letter, telling me that they have "dozens more scripts" to show me (yikes – I barely have time to read their letter), not understanding what is selling in the marketplace and trying to work within that world. Calling multiple times a week or even a day, and getting put out with my assistant if I haven't returned calls, etc. I know this is hard for people who are outside this business to maybe understand, but – we are SWAMPED with our own clients, with their material, with talking on the phone non stop all day with potential buyers, etc. The very LAST thing I might do in a given day is spend a few minutes looking at potential clients. I only have a few seconds to look at a letter

to get the gist of what it is they have. If it takes too long or is too complicated –
I just go to the next letter. I personally never take phone calls from potential
writers – I just don't have time.

**On the average, how many screenplay submissions does your agency receive
per year? Of that number, how many of them actually get made into movies
for film or television?**
Conservatively probably 100-200 a week – I guess that's around 10,000 a year
– oh – I just made myself feel a little more tired. How many of those submissions
get made into TV per year? Well, if we are talking about how many submissions
from outside writers that come into our office – how many of those might be
made into something in a year – I would say that in the time I have been an agent
– 13 years – I have only ever gotten one script from an outside, brand new
writer that got made into a movie. As an agency we have had lots of scripts,
etc., get made into movies every year, but that is a different question. I would
say that I might take on as new clients based on a query letters... maybe three
to five people a year.

**Complete this sentence. The difference between a good script and a great
script is...**
really good, believable, relatable characters.

**With so much controversy surrounding ageism in the film industry and
its favoritism toward the young, how can an over-30 writer break in and
find success?**
The feature market and even the hour drama market place is less fraught with
ageism – and I think to a degree – people sometimes use that more as an excuse
–for not succeeding. The comedy – sitcom market place seems to like younger
writers but we have been able to put people in their 30s and up on various series.
It all depends on the writing. It has to be fresh and reflective of the kind of writing seen on a particular show. I also think people over 30 might be able to lean
on their relationships – people they know to try to help get in through the door.
The longer you have been around town, the more relationships you have.

In concert with the above question, why is age a factor at all in a profession where the artistic creator is a virtually invisible member of the process?

It shouldn't be — but I think what happens in the series world where people work as a group, and when the head writers are a particular age — they tend to look for people with similar age-related experience — so sometimes its not how old someone is — it's how old someone acts — and thinks and that can be reflected in his or her writing. Again in the feature and long-form market — I really haven't seen age being a factor at all. I have a client who is 80 years old and we just made a deal for an MOW for him. But this guy really knows his market, he has been around for a long time and he has refused to grow stale or rest on his laurels.

Adaptations of "proven" commodities such as published novels and produced stage plays would seem to represent a lower financial risk for a studio than optioning an original work by an "unproven" writer. That said, are adaptations a more viable route for gaining an entry into show biz than pitching something previously untested on a readership or audience?

I have certainly had better luck with writers who have the rights to a novel or true story — in terms of pitching. If the story is important or something that an audience would want to see — like Kobe Bryant's inside story or whatever, then that could sell easily. Stage plays that have gotten well reviewed are a good entrée also for a writer trying to break in. Just make sure that you have the rights to sell it — and on paper and clearly. I would not advise writers to adapt a novel or something they don't have the rights to.

There's certainly no shortage of films out there that are light on plot, big on CGI, and totally devoid of characters to cheer for. And yet, they continue to get optioned and produced. What do you think accounts for that?

It's the event nature of a film like *The Mummy* — the concept sells itself. And there will be video games, etc., all coming from it — its sort of really a grand marketing scheme. They are called "ride" films — because you can imagine the amusement park ride that would be created based on it. Very often the scripts for these movies start off pretty solid — but somewhere along the way — all the FX squeeze out the plot. I think these movies are also targeting the 15-year-old male audience — who really isn't interested in thinking about anything too deeply.

Do today's films demand more or less from actors compared to 30 years ago? How can aspiring screenwriters use that comparison to write the kind of roles that a Brad Pitt or a Reese Witherspoon would want to play?
I don't know — if films are more or less demanding — but aspiring screenwriters should have certain people in mind as they write characters. Even if Reese never gets the script — people in Hollywood will say it's a script for a Reese Witherspoon/Kate Hudson type. In this town if you showed up with a script that was for a Kate Hepburn type — everyone would stare at you blankly — and wonder if you meant it was a movie for their grandmothers.

Just as e-books arose in response to the increasing exclusion of mid-list authors by New York publishers, more and more indie film companies seem to be emerging as a way to attract writers whose work doesn't fit a mainstream definition. From your perspective, do you see this trend as one that will subliminally redefine how major studios make movies in order to court the indie audience market share? Rephrased, will the tail eventually wag the dog or will the dog continue to wag the tail?
I actually think that the tail does in a very slow way wag the dog already now. It is always the indie market that comes up with the freshest, coolest stuff – and the big studios sort of take the ball and run with it and over do it for a few months or years until the indie market comes up with the next fresh thing. *Movies like Sex, Lies, and Videotape* or *Four Weddings and a Funeral* or *The Full Monty* were all indie movies and had an impact on what the market place thought would work.

If you could have been the agent for any movie ever made, which one would it be and why?
That is a really hard question — there are so many great movies. I bet that finally getting *Forrest Gump* made must have been highly satisfying. It took something like 10 years to finally get that to the screen. *Rainman*, I've heard was hard to get made — but was a great movie. I have a number of scripts that are my absolute favorites that I have been working on selling for years — just knowing in my heart they would be terrific movies. Unfortunately, as I look deeply inward —

most of the things I've sold — I liked — but the projects usually sold for other reasons — they were really commercial, or the right place and time kind of thing.

Last but not least, what's your advice for newcomers trying to break into the industry with their first scripts?
I would try to find a small producer who is interested — as opposed to going to the bigger studios or even agencies — there are lots of small hungry producers looking for good material who would be happy to read your script. Then LISTEN to what they say, in fact listen to what everyone says to you about your script. And try to get your ego out of the way long enough to see if there are ways to improve it. I feel if your script is not getting incredible feedback from people — like — this is really great — one of the most exciting, funny, sad, action packed, etc., scripts I have ever read — if your script is not getting that kind of feedback — then you need to go back to rewriting.

Take writing classes from writers who have produced work — you really, really, really need to get that script right before you show it around town. Because if it is not up to snuff — then your chances of their reading your next script have dropped dramatically. If it's well written but not what they are looking for — at least the door is still open to come in with something else.

Know your market — but also try to look a little ahead. What kind of movies do you want to see? Are your tastes commercial? You have to remember that it is so expensive to make a movie — there has to be some commercial value to it. Most projects that I reject — are just not commercial. I can't imagine zillions of people wanting to tune in or pay 10 bucks to see it. But every now and then someone comes along who has thoughtfully examined the various marketplaces — looked into her own heart and found a story that fits — and then when she pitches it or writes it — it makes sense and it sells! You may love sandals — and have boxes full of them — but you can't sell them in Alaska in December. I imagine fur coats don't sell too well in Hawaii in July. So be smart, know your craft — and — oh — keep trying. If one script doesn't sell — then write another — and then another. And then another.

CHAPTER 18 | THEY SHOOT MOVIES, DON'T THEY?

Dear Ms. Jones:

The logline of your crime drama, "Galahad's Closet," sounds interesting. Please call our Beverly Hills office on Monday to set up an appointment for further discussion.

Yikes!

Upon receipt of such a letter, you're probably going to feel a lot like Kermit the Frog and Company as their journey finally brings them to the inner sanctum of a movieland mogul (*The Muppet Movie*). Will that cigar-chomping producer in the big chair send for his secretary to type up the Standard-Rich-and-Famous-Contract? Or will you get summarily booted back to your lily pad in the swamp?

We're ready for our close-up, Mr. Welles. Getting your movie idea into the hands of a movie mogul takes perseverance, networking, good timing, and the support and encouragement of your friends. (The Muppet Movie, Henson Associates, 1979)

Relax. Your angst regarding either scenario is probably premature. Besides, if you've done your homework on how to prepare for these meet-and-greets — as well as having a basic understanding of how the production process works — you'll be putting your best script forward.

SPEED-DATING YOUR WAY TO CINEMA SUCCESS

Pitch sessions are the Tinseltown equivalent of speed-dating. Or so my husband pointed out after he overheard a conversation in which I was trying to dissuade a client from foisting her entire manuscript on me. "Things really get cooking by page 55," she kept insisting. "You're not giving it a chance by only reading the beginning."

The whimsical correlation he made to the accelerated pace of today's singles scene was something I'd never considered — speed-dating being a radically alien concept to me anyway. What's the mega-rush, I've wondered, having grown up and dated in an era when couples used to actually invest quality time in getting to know each other. The approach I used in some of my early attempts at writing, in fact, followed that same leisurely, onion-layer-peeling strategy. (Fortunately for my career, an editor tactfully explained that it's all right for Art to imitate Life just as long as the Art version happens a lot faster.)

Once I began to analyze his observation, however, there's a lot of similarity. Just as it's important for the first 10 pages of your screenplay to resonate with wit and seasoned brilliance, your first 10 minutes of an actual, in-person pitch need to be compelling enough to warrant a follow-up call. Such is the playing field of agents and producers in search of new material. The demands on their time dictate that if it takes more than 10 minutes to warm up to a plot, the relationship probably isn't going to go anywhere. Just like singles bars, they know there are enough other available prospects wandering around that it would be inefficient to linger on the ones that don't arouse any enthusiasm insofar as the delivery of immediate or long-term gratification.

So how can you make your project a desirable "catch" in such a warp-speed market? By applying what you know about the rules of attraction and making both your script and your pitch for it an invitation they won't want to walk away from.

> > DON'T LET YOUR TEASER BE THE BEST PART OF THE SHOW. Will the initial chemistry that ignited over Jamaican music and exotic drinks with little paper umbrellas be sustained after you learn that your paramour's golden tan is fake, that he lives with his mother in a mobile home park, and that he's a compulsive gambler? Probably not. Likewise, a come-hither script which makes bold promises at the outset that it can't live up to in actual substance is going to be found out fairly quickly and discarded. This is especially true of writers who front-load their scripts with all the gadgets, gimmickry, and jokes to get someone's attention and then have no material left beneath the surface to parse out over the duration. As a girlfriend of mine was wont to remark about various men she'd been set up with on dates, "Flashy suit, empty head."

> > IMITATION MAY BE FLATTERY BUT DON'T COUNT ON IT TO SELL YOUR SCRIPT. Have you noticed that most of the singer wannabees in karaoke bars try to mimic the voice and mannerisms of whoever made the chosen songs popular? Unfortunately, we as the audience are not only cognizant of whom they're trying to impersonate but also can't help making comparisons, usually negative. Aspiring screenwriters who have yet to discover their own "voice" tend to do the same thing in patterning their storylines after films which were either box-office hits or are part of a transitory "clone movement" to milk the public's mood-du-jour for action, patriotism, or slapstick silliness. While it's hard to find a song or pen a theme that's never been done, there's nevertheless plenty of room for alternative versions. Let them see from the opening notes that you know how to put an original spin on whatever rendition preceded you in the spotlight.

> WHAT YOU SEE SHOULD BE WHAT YOU GET. A dear friend from the South ascribes to the philosophy that, "Whatever it takes to get a man (or a woman) is what you have to *keep* doing in order to hang on to them." If money were the bait, you need to keep spending. If power were the attraction, you need to keep doing powerful things. If steamy sex were the lure — well, you get the picture. The same theory applies to the habit of novice screenwriters to genre-hop once the stories are underway, primarily because they haven't really defined what their films' genres are, to begin with. If your opening pages promise comedy, your audience will expect it to *remain* a comedy throughout. That's what they came for, isn't it? Compare this to a relationship that starts out with a set of ground rules regarding commitment expectations (i.e., "I'm looking for someone to bear my children") but then devolves into something else (i.e., "I'd rather just be friends"). What if that individual returns at a later date and wants to pick up where he left off? Are you likely to trust him — or a scripted sequel — if the first time left you feeling cheated and unfilled?

> THE FOREPLAY OF FORESHADOWING. For a movie to be successful, it must effectively seduce at all levels, stirring the viewers' senses and anticipation to the point that they just can't wait to get to the good stuff. Like flirtation, however, film foreplay can't be rushed or come on too strong. It is instead an artfully crafted path of foreshadowing that spritzes just enough perfume and shows just enough glimpse of skin to turn the pursued into the pursuer without the former even realizing that the roles have been reversed. Operating within our respective frames of reference, we attempt to *guess* what these seductive signals mean and, accordingly, keep turning the pages to (hopefully) affirm how smart we are. Clues that may not be obvious at the start take on new significance as the relationship — and the story — advances, allowing the quarry

to appreciate the clever manner in which they became inextricably hooked. If your opening pages don't contain a visual or a line that not only flirts with your reader's imagination and ego but will concurrently have profound meaning to your protagonist later on, go back and put one in.

> PROBABLY MORE THAN WE WANTED TO KNOW. Have you ever met someone new who felt compelled to tell you his or her whole life story on the very first date? Makes your head hurt, doesn't it? Not to mention that there's an implied expectation you'll actually be expected to *remember* all these details later on. Authors make this same error in feeling the need to explain how their characters arrived at the circumstances around which the film will revolve and — even worse — expecting us to memorize its alleged importance. Unfortunately, the inclusion of too much back-story (whether told sequentially or in flashback) impedes any forward momentum of the current plot. Bottom line: start your plot at the point of conflict and move briskly forward.

> ARE YOU AS TURNED ON AS I AM? Consider how many people pass through our lives each day without registering a single blip on the emotional radar screen. Customers in line at the bank. Passengers riding mass transit. Pedestrians in the crosswalk at lunchtime. Unless there is something striking about their appearance or actions — or unless they personally engage us with a smile, eye contact, or an offhand remark — we have no particular reason to remember them. Likewise with scripts. Unless they reach out and evoke some kind of emotional or physical response, they are only innocuous words on a piece of paper. Don't trust your own silent reading as a barometer of connectivity. As the author, you're *already* involved and committed. Instead, put those first 10 pages to the speed-dating test of an objective review by people who *don't* know your story. Furthermore, sit and watch them as

they read, making note of their facial expressions and reactions. If you've been successful at compelling each of your readers to ask for more, your script has accomplished the first critical step toward success: distinguishing itself from the competition and inviting a longer look than just 10 minutes.

LEARNING BY EXAMPLE

So what kind of plots hit the ground running, tell us up-front what sort of ride to expect, and — most importantly — make us keep turning the pages? Although each of the following hail from different genres and have widely disparate protagonists, what they have in common is the capacity to tweak our curiosity and make us want to explore a relationship past the initial introduction.

> *Raiders of the Lost Ark*
> *Shakespeare in Love*
> *Dave*
> *Moonstruck*
> *True Lies*
> *Broadcast News*
> *Galaxy Quest*
> *While You Were Sleeping*
> *Murder At 1600*
> *Sister Act*
> *Big Jake*
> *Tootsie*
> *Lethal Weapon*
> *Housesitter*
> *Glory*
> *Time After Time*
> *Casablanca*
> *Reversal of Fortune*
> *Butch Cassidy and the Sundance Kid*
> *Sunset Boulevard*

Acclaimed for its historical accuracy, Glory *is a film about the Civil War's first African American volunteer army and an excellent example of a script that stays "on message" from start to finish. (*Glory, *TriStar, 1989.)*

A PRODUCER'S ROLE IN THE PROCESS

Once a script leaves your hands, how exactly does it become a film? Just like the task of making a sausage, (1) there's a lot that goes into it and (2) you probably don't need to know all the details.

It does help, however, to glean an appreciation for the critical role of today's film producer in ensuring that only the best quality ingredients go into the final mix. Fox Producer David Gorder (*Fantastic Four*, *X2: X-Men United*, *Planet of the Apes*, *Deep Blue Sea*, *My Best Friend's Wedding*) allows us a look inside at what happens to a film once the cameras start rolling.

As a producer, how do you draw the balance between the need for commercial success and the desire for artistic expression?
The objective of all studios/financiers is commercial success, and the primary objective of the director (in most cases) is artistic expression. This almost always leads to conflict. Therein lies the role of the producer: to mitigate the conflict by respecting the artistic wishes of the director but also convincing him/her that

certain creative choices may be wise for the movie's commercial appeal, essentially aiming to get the best of both worlds. You have to be a constant diplomat and do what's best for the movie. Filmmakers are in the business of selling tickets so you must keep the audience in mind, but support the director as much as possible to get his vision to the screen. The producer also has to engage in a leadership role to protect the overall vision of what the movie is about.

To what extent do you get involved in the review and evaluation of the actual screenplay for a project?
All producers on a film generally get involved with the script at some level. It is important for producers to compose story notes and script suggestions for the director. This process begins with a budgetary review of the first draft and continues through production. Sometimes you find that your notes mirror those of the other producers and often the studio creative executives, then you consolidate notes and address the bigger creative issues in the script. You look for potential problems with the storytelling and try to solve them before you shoot the scenes. It really is imperative that all producers read the script and provide notes to some extent, whether the notes are creative or production/financial in nature.

How would you describe the nature of the relationship you as a producer have with the investors who finance films on your recommendation?
There is much pressure on a producer to deliver to a financier, both creatively and financially; so, much of the producer's integrity and professionalism is at stake. Therefore, you try to forge a business relationship based on trust and good faith with the financier first, and then you try to take it further into the creative realm if the financier wishes to do so. Some financiers do not wish to get involved in the creative aspects of filmmaking; they entrust the director and producers they hire.

What is the process that you go through when evaluating proposed projects?
I first ask myself if there is a story to be told. If so, is it a good story that would interest others? Secondly, I assess if the story could be commercial or made more commercial if it's not already. Thirdly, are there interesting and relatable

characters? Lastly, I imagine the approximate budget that would be needed to make the story into a movie.

Once a film begins production, what is your ongoing role with the project?
Basically, once a film begins production, the producer acts as a troubleshooter to foresee and avoid production-related problems that could arise. Every shooting day on a movie set poses a new set of challenges and problem solving. The skilled producer tries to handle these challenges and problems with minimal involvement of the director. It is of utmost importance for the producer not to involve the director in any situations that would divert his focus from shooting the movie and completing the day's work. The producer also continues his/her leadership role along with providing guidance and inspiration to the cast and crew.

What are the top three criteria you use to decide whether to produce a script?
1. Story idea or premise. 2. Characterizations — do you want to go on a journey with the characters? 3. Is there potential for good production value in the story — will people want to see the world in which the story is set?

What role does research (market, economic, demographic, etc.) play in the production business?
This is a frustrating question for many producers because market and economic trends are so volatile and demographic trends tend to be fickle, as well. Often it seems audience tastes change weekly. Some generalizations could be made about the market through research (e.g., there is generally always a market for teen/young adult horror films, action films, and broad comedies) that has remained relatively constant over the years. Basically I find that it's really all about how good of a story you have and if you have told it well on the screen. If you have told a good story on screen, then market research be damned, audiences will see the movie you've made—if it entertains them and they leave the theater feeling satisfied.

From your perspective, what constitutes a "successful" movie?
A "successful" movie is a film that does well commercially at the box office, provides a return on the investment, and has a "shelf life" (i.e., audiences will pay to see it again whether it be in the theater or on home video).

What criteria do you use when considering whether a particular script is suitable for a specific market (TV, straight to video, European, etc.)?
The first criteria is what type of audience does the story appeal to and is there a theatrical market for the story? The second criteria is the screenwriting. If the script tends to be simple in its structure and the characters more generally written, it is probably more suitable for TV. Straight-to-video films are usually those films which are geared to a particular market niche and are inexpensively made.

What opportunities do independent filmmakers present to you as a producer? To what do you attribute the apparent increase in independent filmmaking?
Independent filmmakers are bigger risk takers and, therefore, you are more apt to get a complex or controversial story made into a movie. Also directors on independent films have a bit more creative freedom since the studio is not second guessing their artistry and storytelling abilities for a mass audience. More independent films are being made today because studios are unwilling to take financial risks associated with controversial, complex, or unproven subject matter. Studios want to finance films they are fairly sure will attract a broad audience and that have built-in market recognition (e.g., *The Hulk*, *Spider-Man*, remakes of classic films like *Planet of the Apes*, hit TV series, video games, cartoons, etc.). This is why most character-driven drama and innovative films being released today are independently made. The financial risk is lower because they are usually less costly to produce.

What role do you as a producer play in the release and distribution of a film? If the decision is made not to release a film, or to release a film directly to video rather than through theaters, how does that affect the investors who financed the film, and do you or the investors have any say in such decisions?

You try to sell your movie to a distributor as best you can by building interest and holding screenings, and generally convincing them there is a commercial audience for the film, but if they don't like it, there is not much you can do to change it at that point without spending "fix it" money in postproduction, re-editing, etc. You must do what is best for all investors involved, even if that means foregoing a theatrical release for direct-to-video. The longer the film is in the can and not bought and distributed, the harder it is to make money on the film. The law of diminishing returns begins to apply. If there is no promise of a theatrical release, the returns will usually be lower.

How do you maintain a comfort level about the timeliness of a project, given the length of time between accepting the project and the film's release, considering today's rapidly changing political and cultural environment?

A producer on a studio picture has very little control over the timeliness of a movie's release or release date. There are too many extraneous factors which undermine the ability of a producer or studio to target a release date which makes the film timely in the cultural and political environment. Sometimes incredible events lead to unplanned and ironic sleeper success of a film (e.g., Three Mile Island and *The China Syndrome*). But generally you cross your fingers and hope the film connects with audiences at the time of release. Movies about the atrocities of war usually do not do well in times of war simply because audiences wish to escape what they see in everyday life. The time it takes to shoot some movies precludes them from being released during a relevant social or political time — simply because time marches on and changes occur in the political and cultural realms.

Are there any particular genres you consider lacking in quality script proposals?
The sci-fi and fantasy genres seem to be the hardest genres to find quality scripts. Most sci-fi and fantasy writers get so caught up in creating a world, special jargon, and creatures, that they lose sight of good storytelling. Comedy is another genre in which it is hard to find quality scripts because there are different types of comedy (e.g., slapstick, screwball, satire). Sometimes what I read as unfunny can be made funny by a gifted comedic actor/writer. I read *Austin Powers* before Mike Myers was brought in and I thought it was the dumbest and most unfunny script I'd ever read — but then when the comic genius of Mike Myers created the character and world on screen, it was hilarious.

Could you please provide some background on how you became a film producer?
I started as a production assistant in the production office on the film *My Best Friend's Wedding* and that afforded me the opportunity to work around the producers Jerry Zucker and Gil Netter and study what they did on the job. I was observant and made sure I asked them questions about their work if I did not understand. I was mentored by some of the biggest producers in Hollywood (Ralph Winter, Richard Zanuck, and Lauren Shuler Donner) and aligned myself with them and observed them producing movies. They are the producers who saw the "producer" potential in me, believed in me, and saw that I was serious and passionate about producing and they were able to open the door for me to become a producer. You must build relationships of trust with those who are in the position to help you achieve your goals. You also have to persevere and work very hard and long hours.

Given that hundreds, if not thousands, of scripts are written every year, do you have any particular advice you could impart to an aspiring screenwriter on how to get his or her script to your desk?
It generally helps to know if the writer has sold a screenplay before or has been produced. That will usually pique my interest in reading a writer's script. If they are new to screenwriting and submitting a spec script, I suggest they work on a logical one-page synopsis of the story which reveals a discernible story arc

and interesting characters. I believe that if a writer cannot write an interesting one-page synopsis of his story then, generally, the writer will not be a talented screenwriter and the screenplay will not be worth reading. There are few exceptions to this rule of thumb.

CHAPTER 19 | GETTING TO HOLLYWOOD VIA THE INDIES

Prior to the 1970s, independent or "art house" films were synonymous with the European moveimaking circuit. Sans the financial wherewithal and resources of the Hollywood machine, these flicks were generally low-budget endeavors that colored outside conventional lines and appealed to the "intellectual" strata of society.

This same decade also saw the emergence of underground associations such as the Gay and Lesbian Film Festival, artists whose cinematic voice and alternative point of views ran counter to mainstream entertainment.

Somewhere in the middle were entrepreneurial youth with Super 8s, an empty corner of the garage and a bag of plastic dinosaurs.

As the accessibility of camera, editing, and sound equipment grew, the independent film movement grew with it, providing a viable forum for those who wanted to make the kind of movies *they* wanted to see. The good news for screenwriters, of course, is that they need an ongoing supply of quality material in order to stay in business.

INDIES VS. STUDIOS

By definition, "indies" are companies that raise their own money in order to produce the kind of films they really believe in. Driven by passion more than paycheck, many first-time directors and photographers have honed their craft on independent productions, savoring the challenge and thrill of coloring outside traditional lines in order to tell stories their own way. In contrast, the Hollywood studio system assigns creative decisions to executives and managers who subsequently dictate the style and policies for hired directors.

Where studios have the luxury of big budgets, big crews, and custom-made sets, indies operate with less money, fewer employees, and the grace of community volunteers willing to open their homes, businesses, and property to a film shoot. And although many major stars might decline a role in an indie, just as many more are amenable to take pay-cuts for the freedom to push their talent in new directions and widen their options.

The proliferation of indies throughout the world means that aspiring screenwriters can conceivably find film opportunities right in their own backyards. For instance, each state has a film commission, serving the dual purpose of assisting Hollywood productions on location and maintaining a database of local actors, "tekkies," investors, and writers. Not only does this network benefit producers in search of regional talent, but promotes the word that you — the writer — are available to develop and revise scripts. Whether an indie invites your participation in any actual filming depends on the existence/absence of a writer-director team, as well as the feasibility, resources, and expense of shooting a particular story.

Furthermore, you don't need an agent in order to bring your work to an independent producer's attention — another major difference between indies and studios. Indies typically aren't structured by such formality, nor are screenwriters left waiting indefinitely as committees debate a script's marketability. Indie screenwriters can generally expect to play a more active role in a film's development than they would at a studio, where revisions are often penned by someone on staff.

Nor is it necessary for indie material to have been "audience-tested" prior to submission; i.e., a best-selling novel or play. While studios favor established works that represent lower risk, indies are fearless about pushing limits and thrusting lesser-known projects into the limelight. To use a restaurant analogy, studios are serving up burgers and fries; indies are offering vegetable pakoras and tandoori.

So what will your paycheck look like? If you're a dues-paying member of the

Writers Guild, there are already established minimums in place (found at the WGA Web site) which specifies what writers should be paid for virtually any type of screenwriting. Nor surprisingly, a number of indies request that potential screenwriters *not* belong to WGA. Why? Because it does not obligate them to pay WGA minimums but rather to set their own price for services.

With a studio, the compensation and perks are based on industry standards and an agent's chutzpah. Likewise, an established reputation as an already "hot" author is an influence on the number of zeroes on a check. With an indie, however, the package is based on a compromise of what the producer can realistically afford and what the writer can willingly sacrifice for the joy of getting his or her story to the screen.

MEANWHILE, BACK IN VERMONT....

In a part of the country that's known for its covered bridges, autumn foliage, and maple syrup, you wouldn't expect to find movie cameras rolling. Yet the Northeast Kingdom of Vermont is exactly where you'll find independent film-maker Jay Craven and the crew of Kingdom County Productions/Fledgling Films. To help aspiring screenwriters glean a better understanding of the fiscal challenges and the priceless rewards of making indies, Craven shares his insights on what it's like to work outside the traditional Hollywood infrastructure.

Do you perceive independent production to be a stepping stone to something bigger or is it a destination in and of itself?

Unlike Europe, Australia, and Canada, there is not much of a sustainable independent film industry in the U.S. U.S. indies hope to make their first films as a way to get industry attention and financing. I am committed to working outside of Hollywood, and use independent financing and distribution where I can, but I need industry support and cooperation where I can get it. When I can't, I work to find other means, despite the lack of significant public funding, soft money, tax-breaks, and the kind of incentives foreign filmmakers have. The problem is that, in the U.S., "cultural" filmmaking is not recognized or deemed important. And that's what I do — drawing stories from outside the commercial mainstream. This requires me to seek allies inside and outside of the film industry — and even inside and outside of the U.S. It also requires me to dig even deeper roots into the region as a source of continued funding and distribution. This is complicated by the vagaries of distribution and the bankruptcy-prone fiscal instability of so many independent distributors. I plan to remain independent and pursue the stories that are important to me and have a cultural sensibility. I always look for industry allies and support — and am grateful whenever I get it, especially in the form of well-known actors willing to work for indie wages. I try to make this combination work — and still get my films out to as many people as possible.

With a shoestring budget for PR, how do you accomplish that?
Indies face enormous disadvantages in a movie marketplace where the average studio picture dominates the TV and radio airwaves and can spend $50 million or more in marketing. Indies depend on word of mouth and can't be expected to open "big on the first weekend." Twenty years ago, indies could build slowly through word of mouth, sometimes staying on screen for a year. There is a lot more pressure now to sizzle immediately — and to warrant, even for an indie film, as much as $20 million in marketing support.

The advantage for indies is that there is an infrastructure of art houses that know and love film — and who have built the trust of audiences that they reach through mailing lists and Web sites. But these venues also face tough competition. What we really need here are 800 terrific art house venues across the country that are able to survive and program diverse fare, including good self-distributed films, documentaries, and other pictures that don't necessarily have the current big buzz.

Sadly, there are only about 200 such venues, fewer than even five years ago. We need to build that infrastructure back up, with young people hopefully finding that it can be exciting to do this kind of work and find community support.

Indie filmmakers need to be ready to self-distribute and to play alternate venues as well as theaters — libraries, museums, schools, arts organizations. And to work through alternative press and in small towns where they can often get more attention and find audiences for work that can connect with people there. The job now is to build film culture for a broad range of material. This is a tough job but an important one that will make life more sustainable for indie filmmakers.

How do scripts initially come to your attention?

We receive scripts, but don't realistically have time or resources to select many. We did pick up the idea for *Windy Acres*, a comedy TV series we're producing for public television, through a random pitch. Then, we commissioned the writer, Randi Hacker, to develop a script, which we continued to work.

While we have several self-generated solo projects in development, we are much more able to work with outside material when scripts or projects come to us with attachments — especially with talent or a producer. I then get involved as a writer, director, and co-producer or producing consultant. We need allies out there to help us actually get pictures made. We don't have time to work on projects that don't have that kind of chance to develop. We have three or four projects now in development that have these kinds of allies associated with them. That enables us to build the critical mass we need to move them forward.

Do you encourage participation by the writer(s) once the cameras start rolling or do you prefer to make the creative judgment calls yourself? Why or why not?

I do a lot of writing myself, but I have had writing partners, to whom I turn, as needed, during production. I do change the scripts during production, based on what I'm seeing emerge. I then turn to co-writers or the original novelists, where available, to solicit their input. Ultimately, I've always made the final call myself, since I'm closest to what's going on and use the writing to help me shape what's intended on screen. I like collaboration and try to work with all collaborators, including writers, in a way that allows their unique voices, particular contribution, and best effort come forward. I'm always interested to hear what they have to say.

Tell us about your first production.

In 1988, I adapted *High Water*, a short story by Vermont writer, Howard Frank Mosher. We raised about $40,000 from our existing base of supporters and shot the film in a week, beginning on Halloween. The film came out pretty well, we toured it to 62 Vermont towns — and it won a number of festival prizes.

My experience with *High Water* was good enough that I decided to proceed with plans to make a feature film, *Where the Rivers Flow North*, also from a Howard Frank Mosher story. With support from a $35,000 National Endowment for the Arts grant, my wife Bess O'Brien and I launched our non-profit company, Kingdom Country Productions and spent the next year finalizing a script (with local writer Don Bredes), raising money through a foreign sales advance ($500,000) and limited partnership ($6,000 shares), and organizing casting and production.

Part of that wish list included Michael J. Fox. How did you get him to "yes"?

Wade Treadway, a friend from my Catamount Arts days, was hired to restore Michael J. Fox's Woodstock, Vermont farmhouse. I approached Wade and he gave Michael a copy of my short film, *High Water*. One night, I called Wade from a library screening in Olean, New York. I asked him whether Michael had gotten the video. Wade replied that Michael was there, sharing a couple beers. Next thing I knew, Michael was on the phone. He'd liked *High Water* and invited Bess and me to come to his house for lunch the following week. We did — and began the long process of convincing Michael's agents and studios (Universal and Disney) that our project was viable and worthy. Because Michael generously ran interference for us at each stage — and invested modestly in the film — we were able to make it happen. This helped us get our foreign rights advance which was crucial to making the film.

The rest of the cast and crew came through Vermont connections or personal connections. The extraordinary production designer David Wasco (*Rushmore*, *The Royal Tenenbaums*, *Pulp Fiction*) grew up in Vermont. DP Paul Ryan also had Vermont connections, as did Treat Williams and Co-producer Mark Yellen. We saw Tantoo Cardinal in *Dances with Wolves* and *Black Robe* and tracked her down.

I'd known Rip Torn a little when I lived in New York in the early 70s. In fact, he played the voice of General William Westmoreland in the Vietnam documentary, *Time Is Running Out*, where I'd shot some footage as a college junior at Boston University. I sent Rip the script in January '92. He called me in June, having finally read it. He loved it, and I traveled to Connecticut to meet with him. He identified with the character of Noel Lord — and worked hard to bring him to life.

Rip Torn as Noel Lord, Tantoo Cardinal as Bangor, Michael J. Fox as Clayton Farnsworth, and Bill Raymond as Wayne Quinn in Where the Rivers Flow North. *(Joseph Mehling/Caledonia Pictures, 1993).*

You mentioned that this script was adapted from an existing novel. What changes/concessions were made to accommodate your vision of what this film should be?

Because the original novel is fairly short, we were able to keep most of the basic story elements in place. There were changes of emphasis; flashbacks were turned into contemporaneous action; and we cut a subplot involving Noel Lord's hunt for an elusive catamount (a mountain lion thought to be extinct). In fact, we spent $3000 and brought a mountain lion to New Hampshire (Vermont officials wouldn't permit it), but the creature lacked the vigorous performance that the script demanded. So we shot some material, and had to cut it. The last shot of the film, next to Noel's gravesite, originally included the mountain lion. I had only eight frames of material for this shot that *didn't* have the mountain lion in it. So, we had to generate an optical where those eight frames were duplicated over and over again, to create the last image. Snow was falling in the scene, so we had to make a subtle dissolve from one loop to another, to blend the snow into itself.

So what's your best anecdote that came out of this particular film experience? The experience of raising the money was both the hardest and the "best." We hadn't raised a nickel by June 1st, although we had the pieces in place. And on August 1st, we committed to production and brought in the art department — even though we only had $40,000 in the bank, and couldn't touch it until we had $400,000.

Bess and I mortgaged our house for the $35,000 we needed to get things going. And the fundraising momentum we continued to build over the next weeks let us break escrow in time and get through the shoot. We brought in some $750,000 during the weeks between August 1st and November 15th.

Fundraising for indies, of course, is always the most challenging aspect of this business because every film comes together differently and with a different set of backers and players. Plus there's always a strong chance that it won't come together. Beyond that, production is the most difficult and most exhilarating because of all of the unpredictable elements. The director's job is to bring everyone's best efforts forward and to keep all of the disparate elements organized and unified in the same film. Even as new discoveries are unfolding, some will be good and others will be potentially detrimental to your vision.

Production flows on adrenaline — long days, cold nights, punishing schedules, and many unpredictable elements. I love it — and work to hang in with every second of it. But I'm always glad to have it over and to retire to the editing room — and the new discoveries that await me. Along with the realizations of what we did and did not fully achieve during those challenging days in production.

Beyond this and despite some difficulties on which I won't elaborate, the best "luck" was to find the unique combination of cast, crew members, and Vermont producers Bess O'Brien, Lauren Moye, and Alan Davis who worked the impossible to make this happen. The stars seemed to align to make it happen — with an extraordinary gift of grace. Every film needs this — the lucky ones get it.

What was your worst nightmare and how it did it get resolved?
One nightmare involved our arrival at our last location for three days of final shooting. It was for our log drive scene, in frigid water. We faced 5-degree temperatures with 35 mile per hour winds — making it effectively 25 below zero. It was snowing and the water was freezing up, despite our need for a water surface. We had to dispatch six crew members at 3 a.m. each day to break up ice — to keep the water available for the log driving action. Then it started snowing, which was not supposed to occur until three scenes later in the script.

We changed the script and used the snow — but we had to extend for two extra days because of the harsh conditions, which slowed the shooting. The crew was ready to mutiny — for good reason. They thought they were headed home after a long hard shoot. We cut a deal with a local motel owner for a place with hot tubs and Jacuzzi. This cut us the slack we needed to finish the shoot — barely.

What do you know now that you wish you had known then?
How little we knew actually helped us. We took leaps of faith based on our vision for the film. If we had known how difficult it was, we might not have taken it on. We were raising money until the very last minutes of postproduction. We had potential investors visiting the set. It never stopped.

Which view do you ascribe to as a filmmaker: Life imitates Art or Art imitates Life and how did that apply to this film ?
I think that both are true. And, as a filmmaker, you constantly work to discover unexpected moments during writing, production, and postproduction — and to remain open to them. I have certainly felt akin to the Rip Torn character many times, as an indie filmmaker — fighting, in a hyper-commercialized

environment, to stave off the extinction of a way of life and culture that's very much a part of me.

Beyond that, my experiences making these films teach me so much — and open me to new and more complex understandings of myself and others, through my ability to re-invent and reside in character and story for years on end — and through the intense collaborations with others in the filmmaking process. In fact, the films yield new and unintended meanings after they're finished, especially through interactions with audiences. Because, for better or worse, I'm present at so many screenings of my work, I get the chance to pick up these subtle and shifting dynamics, as the film comes to life on screen.

How did the film fare at the box office?
We played Vermont preview dates in late '93 and released it in January 1994, kicking it off at Sundance. We self-distributed the theatrical release, backed by $200,000 from our video distributor, A-Pix. We played 212 venues nationwide — got press on *The Today Show*, NPR's *All Things Considered*, *Fresh Air*, *Entertainment Weekly*, *The New York Times*, *The Washington Post*, and many others.

It was a terrific adventure and success, triggering some $92,000 in video sales and TV deals on Disney Channel, Sundance Channel, Encore, Starz, and elsewhere. Problem is our foreign company went bankrupt, leaving us some $400,000 short in anticipated revenue from that market.

What did you do after that?
My next feature film, *A Stranger in the Kingdom* (1998 release, w/Ernie Hudson, David Lansbury, Martin Sheen), was also self-financed through a limited partnership ($1,000 shares, $750k in foreign rights advances, and a bank loan) and self-distributed, theatrically, but it went into the market during a time when Blockbuster and the studios initiated their revenue sharing strategy, which drastically lowered the price stores would pay for rental video, from $65 a unit to as little as $5 a unit.

Most indie distributors, mine included, couldn't handle the shock and went bankrupt. *Stranger* suffered from this radical market shift, which also drove under many thousands of indie-friendly mom and pop video stores. But the film has now been acquired by a new company and is starting to see a second life for itself, especially through the advent of DVD.

My third feature, *The Year That Trembled* (2003, w/Marin Hinkle, Jonathan Brandis, Fred Willard) was produced by Scott Lax and Tyler Davidson at Novel City Pictures in Ohio. They worked on a similar model, raising local money through an LLC ($25,000 units). My non-profit company, Kingdom County Productions, handled the theatrical release. Ardustry Entertainment handles domestic rights and Porchlight handles the international.

What skills, insights, or vision do you feel you bring to the process of independent filmmaking?

My experience as a Vermont grass-roots arts activist is what enabled me to organize, finance, and make these films. Beyond that, my love of film and my deep roots in this region helped me dig into these stories, which are set here. My work with actors and performing artists helped me develop skills to work with actors. The impossibility of the arts organizing in rural northern Vermont prepared me for the difficulties I'd face.

My 60s political activism helped me hone a vision for an alternative to the corporate status quo — and to favor stories that show outsiders who take a stand for what they live or believe — and face consequences which set the terms of their character struggle. My love of history makes me feel comfortable with period stories and the research they require.

My early history with my grandmother, going to Westerns, enabled me to see my Vermont frontier films as North Country Westerns (or "Easterns") where larger-than-life characters grapple with encroaching progress and an outlaw way of life that still endures here. I also love to work with actors and find that each one communicates in a a unique language. Whether I'm talented in this area is for others to decide.

What are you working on now?

I'm planning, during June '04, to produce *Windy Acres*, a comedy series for Vermont Public Television. In the fall of '04, I'm working to complete my trilogy of Vermont feature films, with *Disappearances*, a whiskey running caper set during Prohibition. Kris Kristofferson plans to star, and we're again raising Vermont money.

I'm also involved with several films with other producers, including 1) *Tilson's Point* (a New England fisherman juggles impossible relationships and choices as he faces the end of fishing as he's known it) with Ken Meyer and Jonathan Bernstein; 2) *The Legacy* (based on Guy de Maupassant's 19th century novel, *Pierre and Jean*) with Maxine Flitman, Vinca Jarret and Michel Shane; and 3) a film based on French crime writer Georges Simenon's novel, *The Fugitive*.

You are also the driving force behind a dynamic program that helps train the next generation of young screenwriters, actors, and filmmakers. How did it get started and what kind of results do you see with your students?

We started Fledgling Films in 1997. For years, we'd seen teenagers contact us, wanting to find a way they could participate in our work. Fledgling Films is set up to support them in making their own films, as writers, actors, directors, and behind-the-scenes filmmakers. We stage an annual summer Institute where kids work collaboratively, in groups, to make a half-dozen films, based on scripts or short stories we find during a several month search each year.

The idea here is to demystify media and encourage kids to express original ideas rooted in their own imaginations and experiences; to help them work with others in a demanding and cooperative environment; to let them experience the culture of a film shoot; and to provide the opportunity to succeed and the freedom to fail.

We also stage an annual Fledgling Film Festival each spring, for movies made by teens from anywhere across the country — or internationally. The idea is to simply recognize and encourage this work.

This process is exciting for us. We get to see young filmmakers discovering the joys and challenges of making films. We discover new talent, from among the teen writers and filmmakers, and the college film students who work as mentor/interns. We also participate in an annual production cycle, which hones our own thinking, especially in ways we can streamline and economize in our own work.

Last but not least, what's your advice to writers who want to break into the independent filmmaking market?
The best advice I can offer is to simply make movies. Get together with your friends and work to tell stories and create images using digital cameras. Show your films to anybody you can assemble to watch them. Make mistakes. Learn from them. Develop a vision. Try some self-distribution. Figure out if this is what you like to do — knowing that it will be extremely competitive and frustrating — and exhilarating.

Beyond that, I'd encourage aspiring filmmakers to help build film culture where they live. Help organize a local screening series; volunteer to work with a local art house, film festival, or arts organization, where you can encourage them to program films as part of their work. It's a great way to support other filmmakers; to learn about many diverse kinds of film; and to immerse yourself in a vibrant film culture, which is essential to building an independent future for dynamic, diverse, and original media.

AUTHOR NOTE: Further information on Kingdom County Productions and Fledgling Films can be found at *www.kingdomcounty.com* or by calling 802-592-3190. Craven also teaches film studies at Marlboro College.

CHAPTER 20 | THE COMPETITIVE EDGE

Everyone loves a winner. Especially production companies who look to screen-writing competitions as a resource for new material. Should you pay fees to enter a script contest? Who are the judges? Will you get feedback whether you win or lose? Such are the questions you'll want to ask when you get ready to put your work up against total strangers in a competitive forum.

WHY YOU SHOULD ENTER

The obvious enticement for you to participate in such contests is the fact that new scripts are actually being *asked* for, as opposed to the customary pitching route of writing copious letters, making telephone calls, and knocking on doors to see if someone, anyone might like to read your story. With certain exceptions (i.e., regional/membership restrictions or a direct association with the sponsor), they are also open to everyone and are well publicized via the Internet and film industry trade magazines.

The prizes awarded are as varied as the type of material being sought and range in value and prestige from a nice chunk of change and/or an option agreement (Hurrah!) to a cheesy certificate and complimentary emory board (Oh). Somewhere in between are scriptwriting software packages, agency representa-tion, expense-paid conferences, mantle-worthy awards, screenwriting books, and professional consultations.

And remember this: although your lack of experience, credits, and representation could preclude you from getting a studio exec to even read an unsolicited letter, your participation in a studio-sponsored script contest will assure that your material is reviewed, judged, and maybe even selected!

WHAT IT WILL COST YOU

There is a lot of latitude in terms of entry fees, the bulk of which go toward administrative processing costs (i.e., PR, postage, photocopying), reimbursing the judges for readings/critiques, and paying for the actual prize packages.

There is also a recent trend whereby some competitions waive a fee in lieu of the entrants assuming the role of preliminary judges themselves. They are further structured so that (1) writers won't be rendering opinions on scripts that are in the same competition category as their own and (2) "test" questions at the end of each reading ensure that the material was actually read.

While your wallet and wits will dictate how many contests you decide to enter, those that provide some kind of feedback on your work are generally worth the cost of admission. Be sure to keep a copy of your entry form, too; you can deduct the contest fees on your income taxes as writing expenditures, along with membership dues, subscriptions, and supplies.

The following sampler of competitions gives you an idea of what's out there, what's in the offing, and what you can expect to pay.

> ACCOLADES/TV & SHORTS COMPETITION
2118 Wilshire Blvd.
Suite 160B
Santa Monica, CA 90403
310-576-6026 (fax)
Web: *americanaccolades.com/AccoladesTV.html*
Designed to provide an outlet for emerging talent and undiscovered screenplays in an increasingly impenetrable industry. Finalist judges include agents, managers, and other industry executives. All finalists receive comments on their material from the Academy Writers Clinic (valued at $120) and possible representation.
Entry fee $35/$45/$55 (based on date of submission)

> **SAMUEL GOLDWYN WRITING AWARDS**
Awards Coordinator:
UCLA School of Theatre, Film and Television
103 East Melnitz Hall
Box 951622
Los Angeles, CA 90095-1622
310-206-6154 (voice) 310-206-1686 (fax)
E-mail: *chernand@tft.ucla.edu*
Open to graduate and undergraduate students of the
University of California.
Entry fee: None

> **20/20 SCREENWRITING CONTEST**
3639 Malibu Vista Drive
Malibu, CA 90265
310-454-0971 (voice) 310-573-3868 (fax)
Web: *www.lets-do-lunch.com*
E-mail: *bonnies@lets-do-lunch.com*
To discover great screenplays in order to get them placed with
WGA Signatory agents and into the hands of producers. If a
screenplay hasn't established itself by page 20, it is unlikely
that it will ever. Let's-Do-Lunch/Screenbrokers' screenplay
analysts, all rated highly by Creative Screenwriting Magazine,
will read 20 pages of each entry. A 20-point criteria checklist
of "musts" for a production-ready script will determine who
will be entered in Round Two for reading of the entire script.
Entry fee: $20

> NICHOLLS SCREENWRITING FELLOWSHIPS
Academy Foundation
8949 Wilshire Blvd.
Beverly Hills, CA 90211-1972
310-247-3059 (voice)
Web: *www.oscars.org/nicholl/index.html*
The prize: Up to five $30,000 fellowships to study the craft of screenwriting in a hands-on environment.
Entry fee: $20/$30 (based on date of submission)

> AMERICAN SCREENWRITERS ASSOCIATION/WRITERS DIGEST INTERNATIONAL SCREENPLAY COMPETITION
4700 East Galbraith Road, Cincinnati, OH
Cincinnati, OH 45236
513-531-2690 ext.1328
Web: *www.goasa.com*
E-mail: *competitions@fwpubs.com*
To assist and recognize screenwriters through networking, educational seminars and industry connections. Competition is judged by professional representatives of the film and screenwriting community.
The Grand Prize Winner receives $5,000 cash and a trip to the 2004 ASA International Screenwriters Conference, including free conference registration, and four days and three nights accommodations, airfare within the U.S. and airport transfers.
Entry fee: $40/$50 (ASA members/non-members)

ARE THESE GUYS FOR REAL?
Judges of screenwriting contests are usually listed generically (i.e., "an esteemed panel of agents, producers, and writers") rather than by their real names. This is done for two reasons: (1) to protect the judges' privacy and (2) to cover those occasions when the judging team hasn't been fully assembled prior to the press release announcing the contest. Even if actual names are used and he or she just

happens to be someone with whom you have had prior communication, contest protocol forbids any outside contact or inquiries during the duration of the contest.

As far as whether specific contests and sponsors are legitimate, I always advise clients to gravitate toward those which have operated for at least three years. That's not to say that brand new competitions don't have merit or credibility, but if their entry fees are on the high side, their submission address is a post office box outside of California or New York, and you've never heard of their work, you may want to exercise caution before pulling out your checkbook.

It's also wise to ask around if in doubt on whether a contest is worth your time, for certainly among the widespread community of aspiring screenwriters someone out there will be able to offer you advice. In addition, MovieBytes (*www.moviebytes.com*) has a "report card" component of their contest link that allows you to post comments of your own, as well as read what others have had to say about specific competitions.

HOW TO INCREASE YOUR CHANCES OF WINNING

> Follow the instructions! Each time I've been called upon to judge a script competition, it never ceases to amaze me how many entrants assume that the rules apply to everyone except themselves. They will exceed the mandated page length, submit inappropriate material, include chatty testimonials from their friends and relatives, ignore all the standardized format requirements, and send periodic revision pages that they expect the judges to insert in the right place. If you're going to go to the trouble of entering your work for competition, remember that the instructions have been laid out for two reasons: (1) To establish an even playing field for all participants. Dull a concept as conformity may seem, it enables judges to focus on the content that's between the covers rather than get distracted by an economic and creative disparity in packaging.

(2) To reduce the number of scripts they have to sit down and read. A person who can't abide by a few basic rules isn't going to be someone they want to work with for the long-term. Hence, those scripts that blatantly ignore the requested guidelines are eliminated right off the top.

> Your script is your calling card. Not so very long ago, I received in the mail a "personal" invitation from a fledgling publishing house asking whether I'd like them to publish one of my novels. They even went so far as to identify it by its correct title and mention they had been enthusiastically referred to me by someone else. Knowing this much, of course, it shouldn't have been that hard for them to figure out that the book was *already* published. Nor should it have been that difficult for them to put together a better come-on than a plain white postcard upon which the sender had Scotch-taped both the return and delivery addresses. The flip-side of the card — the introduction to the company itself — was typed on a manual typewriter (yes, such things still exist) which hadn't seen a ribbon-change in eons. Okay, I thought, maybe their secretary had been hit by a bus, the latest order for letterhead was delayed at the printer's, and the sender suddenly found himself in a rolling blackout with only a flashlight and a rusty Underwood by which to craft his plucky note to moi. "For the start-up fee of only $1,000," he promised, he would put my book in print and let me keep a whopping 10% of every copy sold. I wrote back and asked why I should fork over $1,000 to someone who couldn't put together a decent postcard of introduction. How did I know, for instance, that they wouldn't type my whole book with the same ribbon, xerox a few copies on cheap paper, and throw it together with a rubberband? Their response: "Well, obviously the finished product will be perfect. We were just trying to save ourselves a little time and money at the front end and cut to the chase." The lesson here: You never

get a second chance to make a good first impression, no matter *how* much time and money you're trying to save.

> Enter early instead of waiting until the last day of the contest. The same psychology of theatrical auditions curiously applies to the order in which scripts are read; those seen first tend to set a precedent for those that follow. Toward the end, the judges are more rushed and impatient just to finish up and go home. Suffice it to say, a lot of scripts begin to look exactly the same after a certain point.

> Fill out the required releases and contest forms legibly and in black or blue ink. This isn't the time to show what a maverick you are by dazzling them with bright pink or neon green.

> Include the contest fees in the same envelope with your entry forms and the script. (You'd be surprised how many people forget to do this and mail the money as an afterthought.) Your check should be paper-clipped or stapled to the entry form, not submitted loose where it could accidentally flutter out of the envelope and fall behind a credenza.

> In the event you move or change your phone number during the competition period, let the contest officials know that via mail. If their letter of congratulations comes back returned or they call only to hear the message that your number has been disconnected, it's a lot less work for them to simply award the prize to someone else than to try to track down your whereabouts.

CONCLUSION | PLAYING TO YOUR STRENGTHS

If there's a broken heart for every light on Broadway, you can just imagine what the stats are for Tinseltown. Nevertheless, it hasn't dimmed the hope that burns within every writer who has something to say and who has chosen film as the medium in which to say it. Nor has the passage of a century diminished the ripple of excitement that courses through a cinema audience each time the houselights go down. From the Holland Brothers' Kinetoscope Parlor of 1894 to the most high-tech multiplex down your neighborhood street, they are there for one thing: to see a good story that will give them their money's worth.

After finishing this book, there's no reason in the world that next story can't be yours. Now that you've learned what it takes to get an idea from script to screen, all that remains is to draw upon the energy of your most valuable resource: You.

Tape the following list to your mirror, incorporate these simple habits into your daily routine, and — to quote Sir Winston Churchill — "Never, never, never give up." Success, after all, is sometimes just a matter of outlasting the competition.

> **OBSERVE.** Every morning that you get up, there's a world of free material that is already waiting for you. Train yourself to keep your eyes and ears open to it. Whenever you leave your house, whether it is to go to work or just run an errand, remember that, to the screenwriter, nothing is mundane. Life is a story and every life is a *different* story. As you watch and observe the human condition, you will discover the many common threads that bind us together and how these threads are woven together into hundreds of successful scripts every year.

> **NETWORK.** Talk about your craft, take classes, pursue leads and opportunities to be around moviemakers. To be a successful contributor to this industry, you must be able to communicate, to send a message with broad appeal in a unique voice. This cannot be done in a vacuum. To communicate with people through the medium of film requires you to be able to communicate with people *as* people. No amount of gimmickry or gadgetry can compel audiences to take the trip to the theater or video store if what is lacking is a story that strikes the funny bone or brings a tear to the eye. In order to accomplish this, you need to "know what you don't know" and seek out the experts who can fill in the blanks of your cinema education.

> **EXPERIMENT.** Think of your writing style in the same way you look at fashion, trying on things until you find what's the right fit and shows off your best features. Look at every piece of paper as a fresh opportunity for expression. Get to know your characters, what they feel and how they behave. Take them out to breakfast on occasion just to become more familiar with their idiosyncrasies. As you get to know them, you will also discover how much there still remains to learn about yourself.

> **REMEMBER.** Reflect on the favorite films you grew up with. What are the images, lines, or feelings that still remain with you, even if it's been years since you last watched them? These memories translate to the same kind of lasting impressions you'll want to create for future audiences who see *your* movies.

> **CELEBRATE.** Get in the practice of rewarding yourself for finishing a scene, working out a tricky bit of dialogue, getting your test readers to say "Aha!" in surprise and amazement. It can be something as simple as a walk, a long soak in the tub, eating a meal off of your best plates — or even treating yourself to a movie. And don't forget a glass of champagne, either. You — and your ideas — are worth it!

POSTSCRIPT:
GIVING SUCCESS A PERSONAL DEFINITION

So how will you know when you've reached "It," that nebulous goal that represents the culmination of years of hard work, rejection, and angst? What if you're already there and don't even know it?

On a late August night in 1971, I was having dinner at a vintage café on Sutter Street in Folsom, California after rehearsals at the Gaslighter Melodrama Theatre. Why is this evening so indelibly etched in my memory? Notwithstanding the fact that my dining companion and summer heartthrob looked exactly like a young Michael Landon, it was also the year that I first got paid to act and to write — two careers that have been inextricably linked from that magical season forward.

I remember making an announcement to my date that I was going to be a success.

"Define success," he replied, nonplussed by the ramblings of a star-struck 19-year-old.

I shrugged, thinking it an odd question. Success, by my limited definition at the time, meant being able to actually afford everything I was putting on my Macy's card. Success meant one day having the keys to my dream house, a Victorian mansion that was located just up the street from the theater where we were performing. For that matter, success also meant Barry Manilow would write an original song and dedicate to me.

"You should write all those things down on a list and tuck it away somewhere," he recommended.

I asked him why.

"So you'll know when you get there," he answered.

Obviously my original list has undergone radical change with the passage of age and the coming of wisdom. I long ago stopped worrying about my Macy's bill, the grand mansion on Sutter Street has sadly fallen into a state of disrepair that not even a dreamer could rescue and — as far as I know — Barry hasn't started penning my lyrics yet.

The one thing that hasn't changed since that summer night is the satisfaction I derive from people being touched by something I've done or said. In theater, it's the affirmation of applause. In novels, it's the e-mails from strangers who declare that my cliffhangers kept them turning pages until 3 a.m. In the arena of teaching, it's the joy of having a student come up after a lecture and tell me, "I've been struggling with such-and-such for the longest time and what you just said about thus-and-so was exactly what I needed to hear."

It's experiences like these which remind me that I reached my goal of success some time ago and that whatever happens now is just icing on the cake. Whether or not I ever have a Pulitzer, a Tony and an Oscar all sharing space on the fireplace mantle has become incidental to the satisfaction of being a catalyst for the next generation of aspiring writers and sharing what I've learned along the way. In the event that you, the reader, become one of those next bright stars as a result of anything you've read in these pages, I'd like to hear from you.

I'd be remiss in a postscript, of course, not to mention what my long ago dining companion's own definition of success was. Though our paths went different ways after the second summer and his enlistment in the Armed Forces, I recall his wistful contemplation of what it would be like to see his name in a book someday. "There's an immortality to things in print," he remarked. "It means that people will always remember that once upon a time you passed this way and made an impression."

And so to Keith Snook — wherever you are — I say thank you for giving my dreams a sense of definition and my words a sense of purpose to all who read them along the journey.

FILMOGRAPHY[1]

Age of Innocence, The (1993) – Daniel Day-Lewis, Michelle Pfeiffer, Wynona Ryder.

Amadeus (1984) – Tom Hulce, F. Murray Abraham.

American President, The (1995) – Michael Douglas, Annette Bening.

Angels in the Outfield (1951) – Paul Douglas, Janet Leigh, Keenan Wynn; (1994) – Danny Glover, Tony Danza, Christopher Lloyd.

Annie (1982) – Aileen Quinn, Albert Finney, Carol Burnett.

Apocalypse Now (1979) – Martin Sheen, Marlon Brando, Robert Duvall.

Austin Powers, International Man of Mystery (1997) – Mike Myers, Elizabeth Hurley, Robert Wagner.

Batman and Robin (1997) – George Clooney, Chris O'Donnell.

Beauty and the Beast (TV) (1987-1990) – Linda Hamilton, Ron Perlman.

Big Jake (1971) – John Wayne, Maureen O'Hara, Richard Boone.

Black Robe (1991) – Lothaire Bluteau, August Schellenberg, Tantoo Cardinal.

Black Swan, The (1942) – Tyrone Power, Maureen O'Hara.

Bowfinger (1999) – Steve Martin, Eddie Murphy.

Braveheart (1995) – Mel Gibson, Sophie Marceau, Patrick McGoohan.

Broadcast News (1987) – William Hurt, Holly Hunter, Albert Brooks.

Butch Cassidy and the Sundance Kid (1969) – Paul Newman, Robert Redford.

Calendar Girls (2003) – Helen Mirren, Julie Walters.

Captain Blood (1935) – Errol Flynn, Olivia DeHaviland.

---

[1]There are many remakes of films. The listed filmography represents some, but not all remakes. For a comprehensive listing of film titles, go to the Internet Movie Database (IMDB) at *www.imdb.com*.

Captain Horatio Hornblower (1951) – Gregory Peck, Virginia Mayo.

Carrie (1976) – Sissy Spacek, Piper Laurie;
(2002) – Angela Bettis, Patricia Clarkson (TV).

Casablanca (1942) – Humphrey Bogart, Ingrid Bergman.

Charlie's Angels (2000) – Cameron Diaz, Drew Barrymore, Lucy Liu.

China Syndrome, The (1979) – Jack Lemmon, Jane Fonda, Michael Douglas.

Christmas Carol, A (1951) – Alastair Sim, Kathleen Harrison;
(1984) – George C. Scott, Nigel Davenport (TV).

Clockwork Orange, A (1971) – Malcolm McDowell, Patrick McGee.

Clue (1985) – Tim Curry, Eileen Brennan, Christopher Lloyd, Leslie Ann Warren.

Coming Home (1978) – Jane Fonda, Jon Voight, Bruce Dern.

Coming to America (1988) – Eddie Murphy, Arsenio Hall, James Earl Jones, John Amos.

Crimson Pirate (1952) – Burt Lancaster, Nick Cravat.

Dances with Wolves (1990) – Kevin Costner, Mary McDonnell, Graham Greene, Tantoo Cardinal.

Das Boot (1981) – Jürgen Prochnow, Herbert Gronemeyer.

Dave (1993) – Kevin Kline, Sigourney Weaver, Frank Langella.

David Copperfield (1935) – Freddie Bartholomew, W. C. Fields.

Dead Again (1991) – Kenneth Branagh, Emma Thompson.

Deep Blue Sea (1999) – LL Cool J, Samuel L. Jackson.

Deer Hunter, The (1978) – Robert De Niro, John Savage, Christopher Walken.

Diary of Anne Frank (1959) – Millie Perkins, Shelley Winters.

Dick Tracy (1990) – Warren Beatty, Madonna, Al Pacino.

Dirty Harry (1971) – Clint Eastwood, Harry Guardino.

Dr. No (1962) – Sean Connery, Ursula Andress.

Easy Rider (1969) – Peter Fonda, Dennis Hopper.

El Dorado (1967) – John Wayne, Robert Mitchum.

E.T., the Extra-Terrestrial (1982) – Henry Wallace, Dee Wallace-Stone.

Exorcist, The (1973) – Linda Blair, Max von Sydow.

Far Horizons, The (1955) – Fred MacMurray, Charlton Heston, Donna Reed.

Fatal Attraction (1987) – Michael Douglas, Glenn Close.

Finding Nemo (2003) – The voices of Albert Brooks, Ellen DeGeneres, Brad Garrett.

Forrest Gump (1994) – Tom Hanks, Robin Wright-Penn, Gary Sinise.

Four Weddings and a Funeral (1994) – Hugh Grant, Andie MacDowell.

Freaky Friday (1976) – Barbara Harris, Jodie Foster;
(2003) – Jamie Lee Curtis, Lindsay Lohan.

Full Monty, The (1997) – Robert Carlyle, Mark Addy, William Snape.

Galaxy Quest (1999) – Tim Allen, Sigourney Weaver, Alan Rickman.

Gigli (2003) – Ben Affleck, Jennifer Lopez.

Gladiator (2000) – Russell Crowe, Joaquin Phoenix, Oliver Reed, Derek Jacobi.

Glory (1989) – Matthew Broderick, Denzel Washington.

Gone With the Wind (1939) – Clark Gable, Vivian Leigh.

Good Will Hunting (1997) – Robin Williams, Matt Damon, Ben Affleck.

Green Berets, The (1968) – John Wayne, David Janssen, Jim Hutton.

Heaven's Gate (1980) – Kris Kristofferson, Christopher Walken, John Hurt.

Housesitter (1992) – Steve Martin, Goldie Hawn.

Hulk (2003) – Eric Bana, Jennifer Connelly.

Independence Day (1996) – Bill Pullman, Will Smith.

In Harm's Way (1965) – John Wayne, Kirk Douglas, Patricia Neal.

Ishtar (1987) – Warren Beatty, Dustin Hoffman.

Jefferson in Paris (1996) – Nick Nolte, Gwyneth Paltrow, Thandie Newton.

Jumpin' Jack Flash (1986) – Whoopie Goldberg, Stephen Collins, John Wood.

Lara Croft, Tomb Raider (2001) – Angelina Jolie, Jon Voight.

Legally Blond (2001) – Reese Witherspoon, Luke Wilson, Victor Garber.

Les Miserables (1952) – Michael Rennie, Debra Paget, Robert Newton; (1978) – Richard Jordan, Anthony Perkins (TV).

Lethal Weapon (1987) – Mel Gibson, Danny Glover.

Lion in Winter, The (1968) – Peter O'Toole, Katherine Hepburn, Anthony Hopkins.

Little Big Man (1970) – Dustin Hoffman, Faye Dunaway, Chief Dan George.

Lost in Space (1998) – William Hurt, Mimi Rogers, Gary Oldman.

Manchurian Candidate, The (1962) – Frank Sinatra, Laurence Harvey, Angela Lansbury.

M*A*S*H (1970) – Donald Sutherland, Elliott Gould.

Matrix Reloaded, The (2003) – Keanu Reeves.

Mummy, The (1999) – Brendan Fraser, Rachel Weisz.

Muppet Movie, The (1979) – Jim Henson, Frank Oz (voices).

Memento (2000) – Guy Pearce, Carrie-Anne Moss.

Midnight Cowboy (1969) – Dustin Hoffman, Jon Voight.

Moonstruck (1987) – Cher, Nicolas Cage.

Murder at 1600 (1997) – Wesley Snipes, Diane Lane.

My Best Friend's Wedding (1997) – Julia Roberts, Dermot Mulroney.

Net, The (1995) – Sandra Bullock, Dennis Miller.

North by Northwest (1959) – Cary Grant, Eva Marie Saint, James Mason.

Overboard (1987) – Goldie Hawn, Kurt Russell.

Paper Moon (1973) – Ryan O'Neal, Tatum O'Neal, Madeline Kahn.

Patton (1970) – George C. Scott, Karl Malden.

Pearl Harbor (2001) – Ben Affleck, Josh Hartnett, Kate Beckindsale.

Pirates of the Caribbean, the Curse of the Black Pearl (2003) – Johnny Depp, Orlando Bloom, Keira Knightley.

Planet of the Apes (1968) – Charlton Heston, Roddy McDowell, Kim Hunter.

Platoon (1986) – Tom Berenger, Willem Dafoe, Charlie Sheen.

Pocahontas (1995) – Voices of Irene Bedard, Mel Gibson.

Pretty Baby (1978) – Brooke Shields, Keith Carradine, Susan Sarandon.

Pulp Fiction (1994) – John Travolta, Samuel L. Jackson.

Quiet Man, The (1952) – John Wayne, Maureen O'Hara.

Raiders of the Lost Ark (1981) – Harrison Ford, Karen Allen, John Rhys-Davies, Denholm Elliott.

Rain Man (1998) – Dustin Hoffman, Tom Cruise.

Rear Window (1954) – Jimmy Stewart, Grace Kelly.

Reversal of Fortune (2000) – Glenn Close, Jeremy Irons.

Rio Lobo (1970) – John Wayne, Jennifer O'Neill, Jack Elam.

Robin Hood, Prince of Thieves (1991) – Kevin Costner, Alan Rickman, Morgan Freeman, Mary Elizabeth Mastrantonio.

Royal Tenenbaums, The (2001) – Gene Hackman, Anjelica Houston.

Run Lola Run (1999) – Franka Potente, Moritz Bleibtreu.

Rushmore (1998) – Bill Murray, Jason Schwartzman, Olivia Williams.

Sabrina (1954) – Humphrey Bogart, William Holden, Audrey Hepburn; (1995) – Harrison Ford, Greg Kinnear, Julia Ormond.

Same Time, Next Year (1978) – Alan Alda, Ellen Burstyn.

Scarlet Letter, The (1995) – Demi Moore, Gary Oldman; (1934) – Colleen Moore, Hardie Albright.

Seabiscuit (2003) – Jeff Bridges, Tobey Maguire.

sex, lies, and videotape (1989) – James Spader, Andie MacDowell.

Shakespeare in Love (1998) – Gwyneth Paltrow, Joseph Fiennes.

Shrek (2001) – Mike Myers, Eddie Murphy, Cameron Diaz.

Simone (2002) – Al Pacino.

Sister Act (1992) – Whoopi Goldberg, Maggie Smith.

Sleeping With The Enemy (1991) – Julia Roberts, Patrick Bergen.

Sliding Doors (1998) – Gwyneth Paltrow, John Hannah.

Something's Gotta Give (2003) – Jack Nicholson, Diane Keaton.

Spider-Man (2002) – Tobey Maguire, Kirsten Dunst.

Star Trek (1960s TV series and innumerable films) – William Shatner, Leonard Nimoy, et al.

Star Wars (1977) – Harrison Ford, Mark Hamill, Carrie Fisher.

Steel Magnolias (1989) – Sally Field, Dolly Parton, Shirley MacLaine, Darryl Hannah, Olympia Dukakis, Julia Roberts.

Sunset Boulevard (1950) – Gloria Swanson, William Holden.

Superman (1978) – Christopher Reeve, Margot Kidder.

Swiss Family Robinson (1960) – John Mills, Dorothy McGuire, James MacArthur.

Tarzan the Ape Man (1932) – Johnny Weissmuller, Maureen O'Sullivan; (1981) – Miles O'Keeffe, Bo Derek.

Terms of Endearment (1983) – Shirley MacLaine, Jack Nicholson, Debra Winger.

Thelma and Louise (1991) – Susan Sarandon, Geena Davis.

Third Man, The (1949) – Joseph Cotten, Orson Welles.

Time After Time (1979) – Malcolm McDowell, David Warner.

Tootsie (1982) – Dustin Hoffman, Jessica Lange, Teri Garr, Dabney Coleman.

True Lies (1994) – Arnold Schwarzenegger, Jamie Lee Curtis, Tom Arnold.

Wall Street (1987) – Michael Douglas, Charlie Sheen.

While You Were Sleeping (1995) – Sandra Bullock, Bill Pullman.

Wild, Wild West, The (1999) – Will Smith, Kevin Kline.

Wilde (1997) – Stephen Fry, Jude Law, Vanessa Redgrave.

Witness (1985) – Harrison Ford, Kelly McGillis.

Wizard of Oz, The (1939) – Judy Garland, Ray Bolger, Bert Lehr, Jack Haley.

X-Men (2000) – Patrick Stewart, Hugh Jackman, Ian McKellen.

X-2 (2003) – Patrick Stewart, Hugh Jackman, Ian McKellen.

RECOMMENDED READING

Bennett, Hal Zina and Larsen, Michael, *How to Write With a Collaborator*, Writer's Digest Books, 1988

Corey, Melinda and Ochoa, George, *The American Film Institute Desk Reference*, Stonesong Press, 2002

D'Vari, Marisa, *Script Magic: Subconscious Techniques to Conquer Writer's Block*, Michael Wiese Productions, 2000

Ebert, Roger, *I Hated, Hated, Hated This Movie*, Andrews McMeel Publishing, 2000

Flinn, Denny Martin, *How Not to Write a Screenplay: 101 Common Mistakes Most Screenwriters Make*, ifilm, 1999

Fong-Yoneda, Kathie, *The Script-Selling Game: A Hollywood Insider's Look at Getting Your Script Sold and Produced*, Michael Wiese Productions, 2002

Halperin, Michael, *Killer Treatment: Selling Your Story Without a Script*, Michael Wiese Productions, 2002

Heffron, Jack and Prues, Don, *Writer's Guide to Places*, Writer's Digest Books, 2003

Herbert, Katherine Atwell Herbert, *Writing Scripts Hollywood Will Love: An Insider's Guide to Film and Television Scripts That Sell*, Allworth Press, 1994

Joseph, Erik, *How to Enter Screenplay Contests And Win*, Lone Eagle Publishing, 1997

Obstfeld, Raymond and Neumann, Franz, *Careers for Your Characters: A Writer's Guide to 101 Professions From Architect To Zookeeper*, Writer's Digest Books, 2002

Phillips, William H., *Writing Short Scripts*, Syracuse University Press, 1999

Robertson, Patrick, *Film Facts*, Billboard Books, 2001

Stubbs, Liz and Rodriguez, Richard, *Making Independent Films*, Allworth Press, 2000

Vater, Rachel, *2003 Guide to Literary Agents: 600+ Agents Who Sell What You Write*, Writer's Digest Books, 2002

Wehner, Christopher, *Screenwriting On The Internet*, Michael Wiese Productions, 2001

ABOUT THE AUTHOR

Former actress and director Christina Hamlett is a script coverage consultant and award-winning author whose publishing credits include 18 books, 110 plays and musicals, 3 optioned films, and screenwriting columns that appear regularly throughout the United States, United Kingdom, Canada, Australia, and New Zealand.

Her degree in Communications from California State University, Sacramento led to assignments in all aspects of media, cable television, and public relations, including the development of her own touring theater repertory company, which she ran for eight years.

In addition to her current work as a grants consultant for Young Filmmakers Academy and as a scriptwriter for the Museums of the Arroyo/Heritage Square, she teaches online screenwriting classes, as well as regular workshops around the country for writers of all ages. She is married to insurance industry executive Mark Webb and resides in Pasadena, California.

Christina can be reached for questions or script consultations via her office at *scriptingsuccess@cswebmail.com.*

CALLING ALL SCREENWRITERS!

Since you took the time to read my advice, I'd like to take the time to read the first script you write as a result of it.

This certificate, therefore, entitles the buyer of this book to a professional critique of his/her feature length screenplay or theatrical script at 50% off the regular price of $450.

Coverage will address the areas of originality, character development, dialogue, pacing, structure, format, budget and marketability, as well as include recommendations for potential screen competitions and independent studios.

In order to redeem this certificate, all you have to do is submit an e-mail with the subject line "CIBAM04 CERTIFICATE REQUEST" to either *scriptingsuccess@cswebmail.com* or *authorhamlett@cs.com*. In your request, please provide the information that is listed below and you will be contacted by my staff regarding script submission and payment procedures.

(NOTE: Do not send any manuscripts or attachments via e-mail.)

1. Name
2. Address
3. E-mail Address
4. Where you bought the book

MICHAEL WIESE PRODUCTIONS

Since 1981, Michael Wiese Productions has been dedicated to providing both novice and seasoned filmmakers with vital information on all aspects of filmmaking. We have published more than 70 books, used in over 500 film schools and countless universities, and by hundreds of thousands of filmmakers worldwide.

Our authors are successful industry professionals who spend innumerable hours writing about the hard stuff: budgeting, financing, directing, marketing, and distribution. They believe that if they share their knowledge and experience with others, more high quality films will be produced.

And that has been our mission, now complemented through our new web-based resources. We invite all readers to visit www.mwp.com to receive free tipsheets and sample chapters, participate in forum discussions, obtain product discounts — and even get the opportunity to receive free books, project consulting, and other services offered by our company.

Our goal is, quite simply, to help you reach your goals. That's why we give our readers the most complete portal for filmmaking knowledge available — in the most convenient manner.

We truly hope that our books and web-based resources will empower you to create enduring films that will last for generations to come.

Let us hear from you at anytime.

Sincerely,
Michael Wiese
Publisher, Filmmaker

www.mwp.com

THE WRITER'S JOURNEY
2ND EDITION
MYTHIC STRUCTURE FOR WRITERS

CHRISTOPHER VOGLER

BEST SELLER
OVER 116,500 UNITS SOLD!

See why this book has become an international bestseller and a true classic. *The Writer's Journey* explores the powerful relationship between mythology and storytelling in a clear, concise style that's made it required reading for movie executives, screenwriters, playwrights, scholars, and fans of pop culture all over the world.

Both fiction and nonfiction writers will discover a set of useful myth-inspired storytelling paradigms (i.e., "The Hero's Journey") and step-by-step guidelines to plot and character development. Based on the work of Joseph Campbell, *The Writer's Journey* is a must for all writers interested in further developing their craft.

The updated and revised second edition provides new insights and observations from Vogler's ongoing work on mythology's influence on stories, movies, and man himself.

"This book is like having the smartest person in the story meeting come home with you and whisper what to do in your ear as you write a screenplay. Insight for insight, step for step, Chris Vogler takes us through the process of connecting theme to story and making a script come alive."

> — *Lynda Obst, Producer*
> Sleepless in Seattle, How to Lose a Guy in 10 Days
> *Author*, Hello, He Lied

"This is a book about the stories we write, and perhaps more importantly, the stories we live. It is the most influential work I have yet encountered on the art, nature, and the very purpose of storytelling."

> — *Bruce Joel Rubin, Screenwriter*
> Stuart Little 2, Deep Impact, Ghost, Jacob's Ladder

CHRISTOPHER VOGLER, a top Hollywood story consultant and development executive, has worked on such high-grossing feature films as *The Lion King, The Thin Red Line, Fight Club,* and *Beauty and the Beast.* He conducts writing workshops around the globe.

$24.95 | 325 PAGES | ORDER # 98RLS | ISBN: 0-941188-70-1

FILM DIRECTING: SHOT BY SHOT
VISUALIZING FROM CONCEPT TO SCREEN

STEVEN D. KATZ

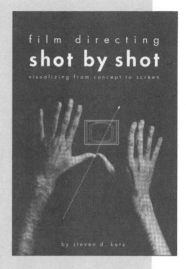

BEST SELLER
OVER 161,000 UNITS SOLD!

Film Directing: Shot by Shot — with its famous blue cover — is the best-known book on directing and a favorite of professional directors as an on-set quick reference guide.

This international bestseller is a complete catalog of visual techniques and their stylistic implications, enabling working filmmakers to expand their knowledge.

Contains in-depth information on shot composition, staging sequences, visualization tools, framing and composition techniques, camera movement, blocking tracking shots, script analysis, and much more.

Includes over 750 storyboards and illustrations, with never-before-published storyboards from Steven Spielberg's *Empire of the Sun*, Orson Welles' *Citizen Kane*, and Alfred Hitchcock's *The Birds*.

"(To become a director) you have to teach yourself what makes movies good and what makes them bad. John Singleton has been my mentor... he's the one who told me what movies to watch and to read Shot by Shot.*"*
> — *Ice Cube*, New York Times

"A generous number of photos and superb illustrations accompany each concept, many of the graphics being from Katz' own pen... Film Directing: Shot by Shot *is a feast for the eyes."*
> — Videomaker Magazine

"... demonstrates the visual techniques of filmmaking by defining the process whereby the director converts storyboards into photographed scenes."
> — Back Stage Shoot

"Contains an encyclopedic wealth of information."
> — Millimeter Magazine

STEVEN D. KATZ is also the author of *Film Directing: Cinematic Motion*.

$27.95 | 366 PAGES | ORDER # 7RLS | ISBN: 0-941188-10-8

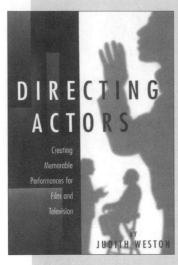

SETTING UP YOUR SHOTS
GREAT CAMERA MOVES EVERY FILMMAKER SHOULD KNOW

JEREMY VINEYARD

BEST SELLER
OVER 27,300 UNITS SOLD!

Written in straightforward, non-technical language and laid out in a nonlinear format with self-contained chapters for quick, on-the-set reference, *Setting Up Your Shots* is like a Swiss army knife for filmmakers! Using examples from over 140 popular films, this book provides detailed descriptions of more than 100 camera setups, angles, and techniques — in an easy-to-use horizontal "wide-screen" format.

Setting Up Your Shots is an excellent primer for beginning filmmakers and students of film theory, as well as a handy guide for working filmmakers. If you are a director, a storyboard artist, or an animator, use this book. It is the culmination of hundreds of hours of research.

Contains 150 references to the great shots from your favorite films, including *2001: A Space Odyssey*, *Blue Velvet*, *The Matrix*, *The Usual Suspects*, and *Vertigo*.

"Perfect for any film enthusiast looking for the secrets behind creating film. Because of its simplicity of design and straightforward storyboards, Setting Up Your Shots *is destined to be mandatory reading at film schools throughout the world."*
    — Ross Otterman, Directed By Magazine

*"*Setting Up Your Shots *is a great book for defining the shots of today. The storyboard examples on every page make it a valuable reference book for directors and DPs alike! This great learning tool should be a boon for writers who want to choose the most effective shot and clearly show it in their boards for the maximum impact."*
    — Paul Clatworthy, Creator, StoryBoard Artist and StoryBoard Quick Software

"This book is for both beginning and experienced filmmakers. It's a great reference tool, a quick reminder of the most commonly used shots by the greatest filmmakers of all time."
    — Cory Williams, President, Alternative Productions

JEREMY VINEYARD is a filmmaker, internationally published author, and screenwriter. He is currently assembling a cast and crew for a crime feature to be shot in 2005.

$19.95 | 132 PAGES | ORDER # 8RLS | ISBN: 0-941188-73-6

24 HOURS | 1.800.833.5738 | WWW.MWP.COM

ORDER FORM

MICHAEL WIESE PRODUCTIONS
11288 VENTURA BLVD., # 621
STUDIO CITY, CA 91604
E-MAIL: MWPSALES@MWP.COM
WEB SITE: WWW.MWP.COM

WRITE OR FAX FOR A FREE CATALOG

PLEASE SEND ME THE FOLLOWING BOOKS:

TITLE	ORDER NUMBER (#RLS _____)	AMOUNT
_____		_____
_____		_____
_____		_____
_____		_____
_____		_____

SHIPPING _____

CALIFORNIA TAX (8.00%) _____

TOTAL ENCLOSED _____

PLEASE MAKE CHECK OR MONEY ORDER PAYABLE TO:

MICHAEL WIESE PRODUCTIONS

(CHECK ONE) ____ MASTERCARD ____VISA _____AMEX

CREDIT CARD NUMBER _____

EXPIRATION DATE _____

CARDHOLDER'S NAME _____

CARDHOLDER'S SIGNATURE _____

SHIP TO:

NAME _____

ADDRESS _____

CITY _____ STATE _____ ZIP _____

COUNTRY _____ TELEPHONE _____

05202930